THE COURAGE TO LEAD

Choosing the Road Less Traveled

ROWMAN & LITTLEFIELD EDUCATION

Lanham, Maryland • Toronto • Oxford
2006

Published in the United States of America
by Rowman & Littlefield Education
A Division of Rowman & Littlefield Publishers, Inc.
A wholly owned subsidary of The Rowman & Littlefield Publishing Group, Inc.
4501 Forbes Boulevard, Suite 200, Lanham, Maryland 20706
www.rowmaneducation.com

PO Box 317
Oxford
OX2 9RU, UK

British Library Cataloguing in Publication Information Available

Library of Congress Cataloging-in-Publication Data

Servais, Kristine, 1954-
     The courage to lead : choosing the road less traveled / Kristine Servais & Kellie Sanders.
        p.   cm.
     Includes bibliographical references and index.
     ISBN 1-57886-260-4 (pbk. : alk. paper)
     1. School management and organization—Handbooks, manuals, etc.   2. Educational
leadership—Handbooks, manuals, etc.   I. Sanders, Kellie, 1967-   II. Title.

LB2805.S541   2006
371.2—dc22

                                                                     2005017781

CONTENTS

EXERCISES, FIGURES, AND TABLES

EXERCISES

FIGURES

TABLES

ACKNOWLEDGMENTS

Our process of writing this book has been a wonderful journey. More important than the destination—a completed book—was the journey itself, which featured great mentoring, modeling, collegiality, humor, and lessons learned. We wish to thank all of the children who have inspired us so that we could inspire others. Special thanks to the pivotal people in our lives: Carol, Angie, Jim, Joanne, and the many family, friends, and colleagues who have supported us along this journey.

INTRODUCTION

To accomplish great things, we must not only act, but also dream; not only plan, but also believe.

—Anatole France

The Courage to Lead: The Road Less Traveled is about dreaming, planning, and taking action. We encourage you to dream about the possibilities during this journey. What roads will you choose to travel? What are you searching for? What is your destination? Who will be your travel companions? What will you pack to take on your journey?

We would like to introduce ourselves to you as your guides on the road less traveled. We have traveled this road as classroom, school, and university leaders. We hope to provide you with travel advice that you can share with other leaders as *travel companions*. As coauthors we discovered the benefits of mentoring, both in our leadership and writing. We discovered that the writing experience was a reflective and exciting journey. Each writing session was an exercise in transforming our lessons and experiences into this leadership guide.

Kristine has been a middle school and elementary teacher, middle school assistant principal and principal, director of field experiences for preservice teachers, and, presently, an assistant professor in educational leadership. The middle school of which she was principal was recognized as a National Blue Ribbon School of Excellence. Kristine has studied school principals and, in particular, transformational leadership as a means for schools to collaboratively create a community of learners. Her most recent work has included the study of the roles, responsibilities, and relationships of the principal as a transformational leader in school-university partnerships.

Kellie has been a teacher for ten years and has been active in many roles as a school leader. She earned a master's degree in educational administration and has served as a school-university partnership liaison between her school and Northern Illinois University. Kellie completed her first administrative position as an assistant principal at an urban middle school and is presently an elementary principal. Both Kristine and Kellie have been active in presentations at state and national conferences.

This book is designed as a guide for anyone who has chosen leadership. Leaders travel many different roads. For some the road from the classroom is one of leadership, while for others it leads to a formal administrative position. Regardless of where you are, this part of your journey will encourage you to risk, discover, and celebrate. As guides we will help you to prepare for, travel, and reflect on your journey. It is a journey each of us has chosen to ultimately make a difference in the lives of children. We would like you to take a few minutes to complete the following activity to assess your readiness for this journey.

To begin our preparation for this journey, we would encourage you to get into shape for your

Exercise 1.1 Leadership Self-Profile

Leadership Beliefs: What are three primary beliefs that guide the decisions you make as a leader?

1. _____
2. _____
3. _____

Leadership Qualities: Identify three strengths or qualities you possess as a leader.

1. _____
2. _____
3. _____

Professional Growth: What is one thing about yourself that you would like to improve as a leader?

_____

Modeling: What actions do you take that model or demonstrate "best practice" for your staff/colleagues? Give one or two examples.

1. _____
2. _____

Leadership Values: What would your teachers/staff/colleagues say is something that you value most as a leader?

_____

Leadership Mission: What would a teacher/colleague/student (select one) describe as your mission as a leader?

_____

_____

Teacher Recognition: How do you recognize or reward successful teachers? Provide several examples.

_____

_____

Prioritizing Time: In what areas do you spend most of your time on a weekly basis as a leader?

_____

_____

Delegation: In what areas do you share leadership? Give an example of how you share leadership or delegate responsibility.

_____

_____

Challenges: What are two or three of the greatest challenges you face as a leader?

1. _____
2. _____
3. _____

Professional Development: To what areas of learning as a leader would you like to devote additional time?

_____

_____

_____

travels. What would a leadership fitness program look like? Much like a successful fitness program, it would begin with a personal commitment, knowledge, motives, and a plan of action to ultimately improve yourself and your quality of life. Chapter 1 of this travel guide introduces a transformational leadership fitness program that includes six areas of fitness for anyone who desires to improve both individual and group-leadership wellness.

The first section of the book provides the leader with the essentials necessary for preparing for the journey. In order to get ready for this journey we recommend that leaders pack some essential items. A leadership fitness plan is needed to help get you in shape to travel. Educational beliefs, the foundation of all that we do, are the next items to include in your suitcase. Each traveler will need to pack a paintbrush and paint to illustrate a portrait of a mission and vision. A map of the leadership standards will be included to help you identify significant landmarks to let you know you are on the right path.

The second section of this book is the journey itself. You will need a leadership toolbox to build and sustain teams. As each traveler encounters different cultural landscapes on the road to leadership, a compass will help to navigate the different cultural terrains. A good leader is able to *walk the talk* and must pack a variety of travel shoes for climbing, walking, and exercising during the journey. A mentoring manual is included to help each leader seek out and determine travel companions for the journey.

The last section of the book takes you home to reflect on and celebrate your travel experiences. Leaders should pack a leadership album to hold artifacts and souvenirs that they have acquired during their journey. Each leader earns travel rewards and will want to return with souvenirs to celebrate the successes of the journey with others. Finally, we suggest you bring along a diary to reflect on your travel experiences along the way.

Each chapter is formatted in a similar manner to optimize learning. The first segment of each chapter provides leadership qualities, guiding questions, and the transformational fitness areas to be exercised during that chapter. A "Sights to See" section provides a preview of the chapter. Each chapter features concepts, strategies, and activities to strengthen your leadership. "Leadership in Action" will showcase successful leadership practices. Within the chapter we will highlight obstacles or doors that leaders may face, as well as possible leadership keys to open these doors.

Transformational leadership exercises are provided that allow each traveler to practice leadership skills. We will ask you to identify artifacts for each essential that illustrates evidence of your leadership. Each chapter includes an area for individuals to reflect on and record leadership travel experiences. As your guides we will share our diary entries that describe some of our personal leadership lessons and reflections. Resources will also be provided for the next time you travel in the area.

COURAGE

Leaders will need courage to choose the road less traveled. Courage, like other leadership qualities, improves with practice. We provide you with opportunities to practice leadership qualities during this journey. The lobster is a symbol that illustrates why leaders need to take risks in order to grow. Initially, a lobster can only grow to the size of its shell. In order to grow any larger, the lobster must risk breaking open its shell, thus becoming vulnerable to the elements around it. As it grows, the lobster once again develops a new protective shell. Eventually, it must determine whether it will again break out of its safe shell in order to risk growing.

The road to leadership will be one of risks and obstacles. Consequently, at times leaders may feel isolated and vulnerable. But you are not alone. Many leaders have made this journey. As you need to, reach into your suitcase, and you will discover you have all of the essentials to be one of the distinguished travelers on this road.

One of the valuable lessons we have learned on our journey is the importance of having fun and celebrating our experiences. We hope this book will be as much fun to read and share with others as it was to write. We are enjoying our journey and hope you will too.

Dear Travel Diary,

During our travels we encounter sights that can instill a lasting lesson or impress on us a defining memory. This was the case for us when we traveled to Atlanta, Georgia. We were scheduled to do a leadership presentation at the National Middle School Conference. Our hotel overlooked Centennial Park, a landmark of the 1996 Olympics. Within the beautiful green landscaping was a water fountain of the five Olympic rings carved in the cement surface. Each of the fountain's rings was implanted with jets, timed to create a breathtaking water show every three minutes.

After admiring the park from the twenty-first floor of the hotel, we decided to take a run one morning and look at it close up. As we approached the fountain we noticed a little boy laughing and wringing with water as he made his way in and out of the jets every couple of minutes. His mother sat several yards away enjoying the display and her son's spontaneous reactions, surprised and showered every three minutes by the fountain.

Our first reaction was to stop the boy from entering the fountain—this is a public display, and it was certainly not allowed or safe for the little boy to be running back and forth into the fountain.

But as we approached the fountain we noticed a large sign. The sign read: "Welcome to Centennial Park. Please feel free to interact with the fountain." We were struck by the unique invitation that encouraged visitors to interact with the fountain.

As leaders we are reminded that when we invite others to interact, we enrich the experience for all.

Kris and Kellie

We encourage you to interact with this book just as the young boy interacted with the fountain. Take time to enjoy the journey and be an active participant in the learning process.

Your travel guides,
Kristine and Kellie

PART I

PREPARING FOR THE JOURNEY

❶

TRANSFORMATIONAL LEADERSHIP:
A LEADER'S FITNESS PROGRAM FOR SUCCESS

Without transformational leadership, the school becomes a ship without a sail, a journey without a map, a compass without a pointer.

—Wilmore & Thomas 2001, 117

LEADERSHIP QUALITIES: COURAGE, COLLABORATION, AND COMMITMENT

Guiding Questions

How will I develop and assess my own leadership fitness?
What are the characteristics of a transformational leader?
How will you exercise the six areas of transformational leadership?

SIGHTS TO SEE

In your preparation to take this journey, we would encourage you to get into shape for your travels. This chapter will compare the concepts of physical fitness to leadership fitness. The success of an individual in both types of fitness is contingent on commitment, knowledge, motives, and actions. We will ask you to reflect on your personal fitness level and then relate and apply these fitness concepts to transformational leadership.

Six areas of transformational fitness, descriptions of each, and exercises for leadership development will be introduced so that you can create your own leadership fitness plan. The "Leadership in Action" segment in chapter 1 features examples of transformational leadership as a tool for both individual and group leadership development. You will also find our first leadership exercises at the end of chapter 1, which include a self-assessment and a framework of a transformational leadership fitness plan.

DEVELOPING A PHYSICAL FITNESS PLAN: COMMITMENT, KNOWLEDGE, MOTIVES, AND ACTIONS

What Is Your Commitment to Physical Fitness?

A physical fitness program begins with making a commitment to change. We need courage to take risks and make changes to improve upon our present physical fitness level. To change our approach to fitness requires us to initiate proactive strategies that help us achieve our desired outcomes over time. For example, a weight-loss program requires a commitment to new behaviors but may not produce immediate results. To commit to new behaviors requires us to desire the potential outcome enough to make it worth the effort and resistance involving in such a change. What commitments have you made to improve your physical fitness level?

_____

_____

What Is Your Knowledge of Physical Fitness?

Physical fitness can be defined as "the ability to perform daily tasks vigorously and alertly, with energy left over for enjoying leisure-time activities and meeting emergency demands. It is the ability to endure, to bear up, to withstand stress, to carry on in circumstances where an unfit person could not continue, and is a major basis for good health and well-being" (President's Council 2004). Considering the number of fitness and dieting books that are on the market today, many of us should have a common understanding of physical fitness. However, fitness definitions may be interpreted in different ways. Knowledge of fitness may include exercising, healthy eating, and rest and relaxation. We understand that when we take time to focus on our physical health we will maximize wellness and minimize the risk of illness or injury. Describe what you presently know about physical fitness:

_____

_____

What Are Your Personal Motives for Physical Fitness?

Once we have attained the knowledge of why it is important to be physically fit, we need to determine our personal motivation for fitness. While many people know the benefits of physical fitness, they fail to identify motives to make the changes necessary to improve wellness. What motivates most people to begin a physical fitness program? Is our motivation to look better, feel better, or perform better? It is important to take time to determine our own attitudes about personal wellness. Once we determine our motives for and attitudes about physical fitness, we need to develop goals and a plan to achieve our desired outcome. What motivates you to begin or sustain a commitment to physical fitness?

_____

_____

What Actions Are You Presently Taking to Be Physically Fit?

In a successful fitness plan our actions should be congruent with our motives. The key components to a successful fitness plan are set realistic goals, pace yourself, be flexible, track your progress, get support, have fun, and reward yourself. Physical fitness choices need to be individualized to fit our lifestyles. Physical fitness can be attained through a variety of activities. Some of these activities include stretching, bicycling, running, weight training, walking, swimming, and yoga. Once a fitness plan is developed, invite a fitness partner to share in the fun and progress. What is your present level of commitment to physical fitness? What does your workout plan look like? What changes will you implement to improve your physical fitness?

DEVELOPING A LEADERSHIP FITNESS PLAN: COMMITMENT, KNOWLEDGE, MOTIVES, AND ACTIONS

What Is Your Commitment to Leadership Fitness?

A leadership fitness program relies on the same underlying principles of a physical fitness program. As leaders we must be committed and courageous in exercising our leadership skills. The fitness-minded leader would be committed, better prepared, and model leadership practices for others. Countless programs and models have been suggested in the search for the most effective means of leadership training and preparation. Transformational leadership is a model we will introduce as a leadership fitness program. This program is not reserved for an elite few but rather is a means by which leadership can be exercised from a wide range of people, positions, and experiences. The ultimate degree of leadership wellness, like a fitness program, is contingent on the commitment, knowledge, motives, and actions of each individual. In what ways have you made a commitment to leadership fitness?

What Is Your Knowledge of Leadership Fitness?

Transformational leadership emerged over the past decade and is broadly defined in the literature on leadership. The goal of transformational leadership is to focus on the commitments and capacities of the organizational members (Leithwood, Jantzi, & Steinbach 1999). Steven Covey suggests, "The goal of transformational leadership is to 'transform' people and organizations in a literal sense to change them in mind and heart; enlarge vision, insight, and understanding; clarify purposes; make behavior congruent with beliefs, principles, or values; and bring about changes that are permanent, self-perpetuating, and momentum building" (1990, 287).

Transformational leadership is a composite of collaboration, modeling, and motivation that influences others to commit to a shared vision. While traditional models of leadership are based on position, transformational leadership is based on relationship building. Traditionally, leadership by authority or position attempts to define a vision and goals but often fails to provide a clear path for individuals to follow. This leadership model enriches the leadership capacity of the organization.

Transformational leadership invites multiple leaders with shared goals and an inspired *followship* all to head toward the same destination. This shared path and common destination is the difference in the success of the organization. The role of the transformational leader, therefore, is one of a path-finder, who effectively defines this shared path and inspires others to follow it. Describe how you are already performing as a transformational leader:

What Are Your Leadership Fitness Motives?

Transformational leadership relies on relationship management to develop and maintain a collaborative community. Experts in the field of leadership, like Roland Barth, John Maxwell, Thomas Sergiovanni, and Michael Fullan, advocate the foundational ideas of transformational leadership. A motive for many leaders is to establish positive and collaborative relationships to define or reshape the school culture.

The adage that "it takes a village to educate a child" illustrates transformational leadership. Each member who demonstrates the ideals of transformational leadership contributes to the relationships and, ultimately, the goals of the village. The capacity and readiness for change in a school culture may rest on the ability of the leader to build relationships with mutually shared goals. A healthy school community begins with a strong leader who is able to support and sustain a collaborative environment for leading and learning. What motivates you to begin or sustain a commitment to leadership fitness?

What Actions Will You Take to Improve Your Leadership Fitness?

Transformational leaders take action in six fitness areas: They build a shared vision and goals, model behaviors and best practices, foster commitment, provide individual support, encourage professional growth, and establish high performance expectations. Leaders should be mindful of these six features and practice each as a means to develop relationships that promote leading and learning. Many school leaders naturally demonstrate many of these features in their daily school interactions. However, the successful leader deliberately strengthens each area to achieve leadership fitness. A leader who makes a consistent commitment to develop these skills is more likely to minimize obstacles.

The following "Leadership in Action" segment describes the six fitness areas and provides examples of leadership strategies that leaders have exercised. These strategies are provided as a means to influence leaders to adopt a leadership exercise plan. How do you plan on maintaining or strengthening your leadership fitness?

LEADERSHIP IN ACTION

The following six areas are the actions taken by transformational leaders. Each area includes examples from transformational leaders.

Area 1

The transformational leader demonstrates a shared vision and goals. The leader facilitates in developing, articulating, and inspiring others with a vision; teachers share in supporting the vision and provide leadership to develop it.

- Vision is established collaboratively and stated and restated; vision is demonstrated and enacted as often as possible through faculty meetings, newsletters, one-on-one conversations, committee meetings, and public events.
- The leader conveys a confidence in the vision and sets attainable goals; success fosters success.
- Quality time is provided to staff for reflecting and articulating the vision and goals.

Area 2

The transformational leader models behavior and best practices. The leader is visible and leads by example in demonstrating positive values and behavior for students and adults.

- Leaders model beliefs, risk taking, and learning.
- Leaders demonstrate best practices in interacting with teachers, students, and parents.
- Meetings model respect for teachers' time, involvement, and learning.
- Leaders recognize and encourage all members of the school community.

Area 3

The transformational leader fosters commitment. Teaming, collaboration, and collective problem solving are encouraged and evident among the staff.

- Participation is recruited and encouraged from everyone.
- The leadership empowers others through shared goals, roles, and decision making.
- The process of change is discussed and developed as a community of learners.
- Tasks are delegated, and there is flexibility in achieving identified outcomes.
- Culture building is supported and sustained.

Area 4

The transformational leader provides individualized support as a mentor and coach. The leader is approachable and knows the faculty as individual learners, just as a teacher knows the learning abilities of each student. The leader is a mentor for others.

- Time and attention is devoted to assist both the veteran and beginning teacher.
- The leaders protect teachers from excessive intrusions on classroom responsibilities.

- New practices are constantly encouraged and suited to each teacher's strengths and interests.
- Teacher efforts and progress are recognized as a means of improving the school culture.

Area 5

The transformational leader encourages professional growth. The leader values the importance of diverse ways of learning and professional growth.

- The leader uses standards to plan and implement professional growth opportunities.
- The leader challenges the status quo, existing assumptions, and current practices to improve learning.
- Staff are offered diverse menus, not mandates for growth.
- Staff have opportunities to try new practices, seek out mentors, and visit other schools/classrooms.
- Meaningful goals and outcomes are attained through quality planning and timelines.
- Budget and support are provided for continuous professional development.

Area 6

The transformational leader establishes high performance expectations. The leader sets high expectations for quality and performance.

- High performance goals are set and attained with leadership support and encouragement.
- Leadership standards are used as tools for measuring educational success.
- High expectations are established for new staff, aligned with the organization's priorities and values.
- Staff are encouraged to take risks to maximize growth and performance.
- Leaders demonstrate an unswerving commitment to a students-first approach.

OBSTACLES AND KEYS

Transformational leadership fitness, like physical fitness, requires a clear purpose, action plan, and commitment if it is to be successful. One of the obstacles that leaders face is limited training and experience, in comparison with the wide variety of needs of each organization. Consequently, each leader demonstrates leadership strategies that are not necessarily responsive to the organizational needs. A leadership fitness plan, on the other hand, is implemented on the basis of the mutual needs of the leader and the organization.

Leadership is about transformation. Transformational leaders build relationships in order to individually and collectively build leadership capacity. The key for the transformational leader is to establish a leadership fitness plan in order to develop and sustain a collaborative community.

LEADERSHIP EXERCISES

We have designed four transformational leadership exercises. These exercises were created to strengthen the six areas of transformational leadership fitness. Exercises will ask you to identify evidence or artifacts of your leadership journey. In chapter 9 these artifacts will be collected as a portfolio to showcase your leadership skills and development.

Exercise 1.1   Transformational Leadership Fitness Program Self-Assessment

Complete the following self-assessment on the transformational fitness areas listed below. Note the areas in which you already have strengths and those you wish to improve or develop. Consider time commitments and priorities while developing your fitness program. We encourage you to invite a fitness partner to join you who shares similar priorities and values.

Vision	Modeling best practices	Fostering commitment
Support	Professional Growth	High Expectations

1. My present level of transformational leadership (TL) fitness includes:
   - TL strengths:

     _____

     _____

     _____

   - TL areas to improve:

     _____

     _____

     _____

2. My fitness goals and desired outcomes include:
   - Goals: _____

     _____

     _____

   - Measurement (How will I know I have reached my goal?):

     _____

     _____

     _____

   - Outcomes (How will others know I have reached my goal?):

     _____

     _____

     _____

3. How will I document my commitment to these goals and outcomes?
   - Prioritized time commitments (How will I keep track of my leadership exercise program?):

     _____

     _____

     _____

4. I have invited a partner to join me in my commitment to leadership fitness.
   - My leadership fitness partner is _____

5. Describe and assess how I am making progress in my fitness plan:
   - Feedback from my mentor and fitness partner:

     _____

     _____

     _____

   - Self-reflection:

     _____

     _____

     _____

- Feedback from others (students, teachers, parents, etc.):

  _____
  _____
  _____

- Family and friends:

  _____
  _____
  _____

6. I will motivate myself to achieve my fitness goals in these ways:
   - What professional materials will I read to strengthen myself as a leader?

     _____
     _____
     _____

   - What professional training will I attend to strengthen my fitness areas?

     _____
     _____
     _____

   - What leadership exercises will I perform to improve my leadership fitness?

     _____
     _____
     _____

Exercise 1.2   A Transformational Leadership Fitness Plan

How will you exercise and develop strength in these transformational leadership areas? Provide examples of a specific activity or action you will take to increase your fitness level as a transformational leader for each exercise below.

Building a shared vision

1. _____
2. _____
3. _____

Modeling values and best practices

1. _____
2. _____
3. _____

Fostering commitment

1. _____
2. _____
3. _____

Providing individual support

1. _____
2. _____
3. _____

Providing professional growth and development

1. _____
2. _____
3. _____

Establishing and maintaining high expectations

1. _____
2. _____
3. _____

Exercise 1.3   Artifact

Identify artifacts or evidence of your leadership fitness. Locate or create an artifact to place in your leadership journey album. Sample artifacts may be annual performance reviews, written communication examples, agendas, professional growth evidence, and written feedback from organizational stakeholders. Take a minute to jot down a few of your leadership fitness artifacts that will be placed in your journey album.

_____

_____

_____

Exercise 1.4   Reflective Practice

What commitments will I make to enhance my leadership fitness? How will these commitments improve my performance in my present role?

_____

_____

_____

Dear Diary,

This morning I headed to the gym to get in an early workout. When I work out, I think of a lot of new ideas and like to jot them down in a notebook. It is a great time for me to reflect on my work and create new ideas for my teaching and writing.

On this particular morning, I looked around the gym and thought about the reasons people work out. Words came to mind such as dedication, endurance, commitment, and strength. I considered for the first time how similar physical fitness is to leadership fitness. I realized that these same characteristics are found in successful leaders. Leaders must be aware of ways to strengthen and measure their own leadership development. I jotted down this new connection and realized that it would become a new way of examining leadership performance.

Little did I know that a visit to the gym would cause me to view leadership performance in a new way.

Kris

RESOURCES

Barth, R. (2001). *Learning by Heart*. San Francisco: Jossey-Bass.

Covey, S. (1990). *Principle Centered Leadership*. New York: Summit Books.

Fullan, M. (2001). *Leading in a Culture of Change*. New York: John Wiley & Sons.

Leithwood, K., D. Jantzi, & R. Steinbach (1999). *Changing Leadership for Changing for Changing Times*. Philadelphia: Open University Press.

Maxwell, J. (2001a). *Developing the Leader within You*. Nashville, Tenn.: Injoy.

President's Council on Physical Fitness and Sports (n.d.). *Fitness Fundamentals*. Retrieved January 18, 2004, from www.hoptechno.com/book11.htm.

Sergiovanni, T. (1996). *Moral Leadership: Getting to the Heart of School Improvement*. San Francisco: Jossey-Bass.

Wilmore, E., & C. Thomas (2001, Spring). The New Century: Is It Too Late for Transformational Leadership? *Educational Horizons*, Pi Lambda Theta, 79(3), 115–23.

2

EDUCATIONAL BELIEFS: TO THINE OWN SELF BE TRUE

What you want to do, and what you can do, is limited only by what you can dream.

—Mike Melville

LEADERSHIP QUALITIES: RISK TAKING, EMPOWERMENT, AND INSPIRING

Guiding Questions

What are your primary beliefs?
How are your beliefs identified, demonstrated and communicated to others?
How do your beliefs support your actions?

Transformational Leadership Fitness Areas

2 Models behavior and best practices
3 Fosters commitment
4 Provides individual support

SIGHTS TO SEE

Beliefs guide us in deciding the roads we will travel on our leadership journey. The healthy school leader is aware of these beliefs and strives to demonstrate them through actions that are congruent for themselves and others. In this chapter we will describe the importance of identifying, demonstrating, and reflecting our beliefs. We will introduce you to an activity in which educational leaders can develop *beliefs*, take *action*, and *reflect* in order to *raise the BAR* for themselves and others.

A second area that will be introduced during this part of your travels is how personal qualities contribute to the actions and success of leaders. Each essential will feature leadership qualities for you to consider in your leadership development. These qualities support the beliefs, actions, and reflections of a leader.

The effective leader demonstrates knowledge, dispositions, and performance as benchmarks of success. A leader's dispositions or qualities illustrate the potential to learn and perform. Within the leadership literature are many examples of qualities you might possess or wish to further develop as a leader. As you raise the BAR in your beliefs, actions, and reflections, consider the qualities you would like to further develop. Some examples are given for you here:

Leadership Qualities

Risk Taking	Influence	Commitment	Integrity	Courage	Caring
Self-Discipline		Problem Solving	Humor	Passion	Vision
	Initiative	Discernment	Service	Optimism	

In this chapter we will incorporate our leadership beliefs and qualities in a process to create a leader's vision, mission, and goals. The "Leadership in Action" segment will provide examples of educational leaders' belief statements. The chapter will conclude with leadership fitness exercises to assist you in identifying your beliefs, actions, and reflections to *raise the BAR* for yourself and your organization.

RAISING THE BAR

Beliefs may be the most fundamental and essential component of leadership. This chapter will examine ways leaders can raise the BAR—to define beliefs, put these beliefs into action, and continuously reflect on their value. When *raising the BAR*, the school leader must begin by discovering the beliefs that are fundamental to their values, qualities, and lifestyle. Once beliefs are established, the leader strives to demonstrate and put them into action. Thirdly, the effective leader continuously reflects upon beliefs and determines how these beliefs are validated and affirmed by others. These three steps will be explored as a process to assist leaders in discovering their beliefs, acting upon them, and devoting time to reflective practice.

One of the first steps for a leader is to become aware of his or her beliefs. This begins with the ability to consciously identify and articulate them. Consider three of your primary beliefs. Write three of your beliefs here:

1. _____

2. _____

3. _____

HOW DO WE DISCOVER OUR BELIEFS?

The first step in *raising the BAR* is to identify what we believe. Beliefs are formed through a variety of interactions from childhood through adulthood. Think about a belief that drives your actions as a leader. Where did you learn this belief? Did you learn it on your own, or did someone model this belief for you? When did you first notice it was important? Beliefs are learned behaviors; we are not born with these convictions. We have been exposed to these beliefs in a variety of settings and through our many interactions with others. Many of us learn our beliefs from childhood events, modeling by others, defining moments, life experiences, and adversity.

Childhood Events

One source of our beliefs is childhood events. As young children we were taught to say "thank you," "please," "excuse me," "you're welcome," and so on. These statements represent the formation of our early beliefs and how we interact with others. Religious beliefs are also instilled at an early age, and they play an integral role in our personal development. As children, our home and religious experiences shape many of the beliefs we carry throughout our lives. How have childhood events shaped your present day beliefs?

Modeling by Others

We learn many of our behaviors by watching others. During our childhood many of our impressions were made by our parents, family members, teachers, and coaches. These pivotal people modeled and shaped many of our present-day beliefs. Who taught us the importance of proper manners, the Golden Rule, and good sportsmanship? Take a moment to contemplate some of the key figures in your life who have played key roles in the development of your beliefs. What made these people memorable? Did you know what they believed? What qualities did you notice and want to develop from them?

Defining Moments

Certain moments in our lives have made a significant impact in shaping the individuals we are today. These are moments that may change or affirm the beliefs we already possess. Dr. Phil McGraw (2001), in his book *Self Matters*, suggests that each of us will experience ten defining moments, seven critical choices, and five pivotal people. What have been key moments that have altered who you are and what you believe? Think of the moment you knew that you wanted to be a teacher. In what moment did you realize that you could make an impact on the lives of students? Think of the defining moments in your life and how these moments have guided you to develop your present beliefs.

Life Experiences

Many of our core beliefs are discovered through life experiences. Athletic activities, educational experiences, and career choices are life events that help to define our beliefs. Many lessons are learned through athletic involvement. Leaders frequently draw on athletic lessons, such as team building, goal setting, and performance assessment. Athletes and coaches embed core beliefs into their personal leadership style. What beliefs did you learn through participation in athletics?

_____

_____

We may look back at our moments as students within a classroom and reflect on how these interactions inspired our present educational beliefs. What do you remember about a special teacher? How did you interact socially with others in the school setting? Our learning experiences inspired many of us to pursue a career in the field of education. One life experience may have been the first moment we stood in front of a class and realized the responsibility we hold as a teacher. How do you demonstrate these core beliefs in your present position?

_____

_____

Career choices are defined through high school and college. These are memorable times that define who we are, whom we will choose as friends and spouses, and the career choices we will make. These defining times ultimately influence our adulthood roles with our families, jobs, and lifestyles. What was a significant event that occurred in high school or college? Who was a pivotal person who guided you to your present position?

_____

_____

Challenges and Adversity

We learn from positive as well as negative events in our lives. We can all cite times when we ultimately experienced success through adversity. It is the strong and persistent person who works through disappointments and learns from them. Consider some of the greatest challenges you have faced. When was the last time you faced adversity? How did this change your beliefs?

_____

_____

Personal Discovery

We encourage you to take a moment and record some of your life experiences that have shaped your beliefs in each area below:

Childhood events _____

Modeling by others _____

Defining moments _____

Life experiences _____

Adversity _____

HOW DO OUR ACTIONS DEMONSTRATE OUR BELIEFS?

The second step in raising the BAR is to consider the ways in which our beliefs are congruent with our actions. Once we have defined our beliefs, we should consider how well our actions demonstrate our beliefs. Consider the three beliefs you recorded at the beginning of this chapter. Effective leaders inspire others to higher levels of performance and development by *walking their talk*. How do we show others what we believe? Would those around you find that your beliefs are congruent with your actions?

When beliefs are demonstrated through our behaviors, we become a model for those around us. If we want the stakeholders in our educational settings to understand our beliefs, we need to demonstrate them through our actions. For example, if leaders believe that all students can learn, they will consistently behave accordingly, and will be seen by others. What actions demonstrate your beliefs? How are these beliefs demonstrated through decisions, professional development, and interactions with others?

_____

_____

Cultural Beliefs

Personal and organizational beliefs mutually influence the development of a school culture. School culture reflects the combined beliefs of its members. When we take action on our beliefs, we influence others and, consequently, the school culture. Ideally, leaders are aware of the cultural beliefs of the organization and demonstrate personal beliefs that support this culture. When personal beliefs and cultural beliefs are compatible, leaders can be more effective and experience less conflict. Core beliefs serve as an internal compass that conceptually points a leader in the right direction. Are you aware of your cultural beliefs? Are these congruent with your core beliefs? How do you act on your beliefs within your organizational culture?

_____

_____

Decisions

Leaders make many decisions throughout their day. Our beliefs are a guiding force in how we go about making these decisions. Leaders need to constantly prioritize where they spend their time and, consequently, the types of decisions they make. Think back to a few decisions that you have made recently and determine if these leadership decisions support your beliefs. What decisions have you made that illustrated your beliefs? Based on your decisions, what would your colleagues say are your beliefs?

_____

_____

Professional Development

Professional development is the action that leaders take to empower themselves and those around them. If we believe that a leader should be the lead learner in the school, then our actions must demonstrate this belief. Leaders are responsible to provide professional development for all members of the school community. Likewise, leaders must seek out professional development for themselves in order to learn and grow. How do you demonstrate your beliefs through your personal and organizational professional development?

_____

_____

Interactions with Others

Through interaction with others leaders demonstrate their beliefs. Leaders have opportunities to influence others through daily interactions. We build relationships with our colleagues when we listen, support, or respond to them. In both listening and responding, we engage in actions and leadership qualities that demonstrate what we believe. Leaders should be cognizant of the ways in which they interact with others. How can you strengthen interactions in your school community? How do you support others through your interactions?

_____

_____

Personal Discovery

How do your actions support your beliefs? How are your beliefs demonstrated on a daily basis through:

Culture? _____

_____

Decisions? _____

_____

Professional development? _____

_____

Interactions with others? _____

_____

HOW DO WE REFLECT ON OUR BELIEFS AND ACTIONS?

Reflection is a means to assess our beliefs and actions. Through reflective practice we are able to affirm or modify our beliefs. Reflection is the report card by which we score and evaluate our beliefs. Effective leaders are constantly critiquing their beliefs, actions, and decisions. Reflective practice is continuous self-analysis of our leadership. Reflection can occur through formal written communication, informal conversations, mentors, observation, and mental processing. Ultimately, leaders must reflect and seek out evidence to determine the success of their actions. The following reflective practices will ask you to consider evidence of your leadership from collegial conversations, feedback, and lessons learned.

Collegial Conversations

Collegial conversations allow us to learn about ourselves through interactions with influential people within our professional lives. The reflective leader will dedicate time for conversations with valued colleagues or mentors. These conversations provide leaders with opportunities to listen and gain diverse perspectives. Collegial conversations create connections by letting others know that we value their time, relationship, and insights.

Margaret Wheatley (2002) highlights the many benefits of collegial conversations in her book *Turning to One Another: Simple Conversations to Restore Hope to the Future.* Among these benefits she suggests that conversation is the natural way that humans think together and acknowledge each other. Collegial conversations affirm our beliefs and action. How have you strengthened or changed your beliefs on the basis of conversations with a valued colleague?

_____

_____

Feedback from Others

Feedback from others affirms or contradicts our leadership beliefs. Collaborative leaders invite feedback from colleagues, mentors, students, and parents. The transformational leader develops relationships and fosters a commitment that maximizes trust. This trust empowers members who share in the goals and commitments of the organization to provide feedback that will benefit the leader and the community. Feedback is provided through conversations, assessments, written communications, and interactions. Leaders utilize this feedback to affirm their beliefs and leadership development. Who are the people within your schools who provide feedback for you? How do you actively seek feedback from all stakeholders?

_____

_____

Lessons Learned

Leaders use self-analysis as a mode of reflection to determine lessons learned. Leadership lessons occur following feedback from others, observations, and actions taken. The most meaningful of these lessons may be the result of adversity or challenges. Self-analysis is introspective and requires time. Leaders must devote time to reflect in order to analyze and strengthen their core beliefs. How do you analyze feedback and lessons learned? How has this reflection strengthened or modified your beliefs?

_____

_____

Personal Discovery

How do you reflect on your beliefs? Take a moment to write down how you have used the previous reflective methods to support your own beliefs.

Collegial conversations _____

_____

Feedback from others _____

_____

Lessons learned _____

_____

RAISING THE BAR SUMMARY

Raising the BAR occurs differently for each school leader. Just as transformational leaders exercise leadership development in a variety of ways, so must each leader determine a process best suited for developing beliefs. Leaders do not have a formula for discovering, demonstrating, and affirming beliefs. Sometimes leaders discover their beliefs after seeing them demonstrated by others. Typically, leaders discover personal and fundamental beliefs based on their actions. The leadership exercises located at the end of this chapter will assist you in determining your fundamental beliefs. When transformational leaders clearly define their beliefs, they model behavior and best practices, foster commitment, and provide individual support.

A leader's beliefs are authenticated by-products of their leadership. These products are evidence of the effectiveness of a leader. If leaders believe they are the lead learners in the school, then evidence will exist of professional growth. What evidence do you have that supports your beliefs? How will you discover evidence of your beliefs?

_____

_____

LEADERSHIP IN ACTION

One strategy leaders find helpful in establishing their beliefs, is to examine the beliefs of others. The following "leadership in action" are beliefs shared by school principals, classroom teachers, administrative leadership candidates, and superintendents.

Leadership Beliefs

Shared success is empowering ~ We need to recognize individual strengths and bring them together in a community ~ The school belongs to the community and the community belongs to the school ~ The school leader must provide a clear sense of vision for its staff and students ~ The school leader will provide an atmosphere that offers support, guidance, and encouragement to build and foster relationships ~ An educational leader's greatest responsibility is to provide every child with caring and competent teachers ~ Leaders have a responsibility to develop the learning culture of a school community ~ Effective leaders demonstrate and recognize the worth of others on an individual basis ~ Integrity for school leaders is the congruence of student-centered values, beliefs, and actions ~ Successful leaders are only as good as those who surround them; they mold, model, and mentor other aspiring leaders ~ The effective educational leader will recognize that parents are the first and foremost educators of their children and that a partnership needs to be developed and fostered between home and school ~ Leaders must be willing to be vulnerable and trust in the abilities of other people and allow those people to do their best ~ Leaders should learn from those they lead ~ The most important belief is our belief in each other ~ Education is a student-driven process ~ Students will be inspired by inspired teachers ~ An effective leader must continually strive to build healthy relationships with all individuals in the organization ~ Inspired leaders build an inspired culture of learning ~ An individual's dignity is essential for learning and growth ~ Celebration of success leads to more success ~ Humor makes the light come on ~ Great leaders help others achieve personal growth ~ To the world, you are only one person, but to one person, you may be the world

OBSTACLES AND KEYS

Leaders rarely learn a method for defining beliefs. Many leaders do not take the time to identify or develop beliefs. We have included it as one of the essentials of collaborative leadership because we have found limited resources written about leadership beliefs. As your guides, we found from our experiences that beliefs are one of the most important ingredients of leadership.

Leaders who take the time to raise the BAR will realize the impact that they will have on chil-

dren, teachers, parents, and colleagues. Transformational leaders identify and demonstrate fundamental beliefs that contribute to a stronger school community.

LEADERSHIP EXERCISES

The following exercises will assist you in developing your beliefs. You will be asked to identify evidence or artifacts that showcase your leadership actions through your beliefs.

Exercise 2.1   Raising the BAR

School leaders are guided by beliefs that are well defined, demonstrated, and validated. Leaders raise the BAR through their beliefs, actions, and reflections. Consider the following three questions as a way to strengthen your own leadership beliefs.

Identify one of your primary beliefs:

_____

1. How did you discover this belief? Place a check mark next to how you discovered this belief.
   - _____ Childhood events
   - _____ Modeling by others
   - _____ Defining moments
   - _____ Life experiences
   - _____ Adversities
   - _____ Other _____

   Describe:
   _____
   _____

2. How do you demonstrate this belief? Place a check mark next to following behaviors that demonstrate your primary belief.
   - _____ Culture
   - _____ Decisions
   - _____ Professional development
   - _____ Interactions with others
   - _____ Other _____

   Describe:
   _____
   _____

3. How do you affirm this belief? Place a check mark next to the actions that affirm this belief.
   - _____ Reflections
   - _____ Collegial conversations
   - _____ Feedback from others
   - _____ Self-analysis
   - _____ Evidence of beliefs
   - _____ Other _____

   Describe:
   _____
   _____

Exercise 2.2   Beliefs and Vision Worksheet

Beliefs
My actions as a leader are based on these beliefs:

_____
_____
_____
_____

Vision
My vision for this organization:

_____
_____
_____
_____

Mission
My mission to accomplish my beliefs:

_____
_____
_____
_____

Goals
Measurable goals to accomplish my mission (specific, measurable, attainable, results oriented, and time bound):

_____
_____
_____
_____

Actions
Specific actions to implement my goals:

_____
_____
_____
_____

Exercise 2.3   Artifact

Identify artifacts or evidence of your leadership beliefs. Locate or create an artifact to place in your leadership journey album. One artifact may simply be a list of your primary beliefs. Other artifacts school leaders have identified that illustrate their primary beliefs are school goals, newsletters, bulletins, or notes from stakeholders. Take a minute to jot down a few of your belief artifacts that will be placed in your journey album.

_____

_____

_____

_____

Exercise 2.4   Reflective Practice

How do your beliefs support your actions? Identify specific examples of your daily actions and how these illustrate your beliefs.

_____

_____

_____

_____

Dear Diary,

This year as a principal my first open house was a success. Many parents attended to meet their child's teachers and myself. One of the best parts of the evening was being the last person to leave the building. It only took me a second to realize why that moment was so important. A year ago as an assistant principal, I was at school for an open house. As parents were still touring the building and speaking with teachers, my principal suggestedthat it would be okay to head for home. Although reluctantly, I followed her advice and we left.

As I drove away from school that night and saw all the cars in the parking lot, I was distressed. I actually cried that night because I felt horrible leaving my students and parents while a school event was going on. As I reflect back on that evening, I realize that the action of leaving the building that night was in conflict with my beliefthat visible presence is so important as a leader My feelings of regret and sadness demonstrated to me the importance of acting in ways that support my beliefs.

Kellie

RESOURCES

Barth, R. (2001). *Learning by Heart.* San Francisco: Jossey-Bass.

Jones, L. (1998). *The Path: Creating Your Mission Statement for Work and for Life.* New York: Hyperion.

Maxwell, J. (1993). *Developing the Leader within You.* Nashville, Tenn.: Injoy.

Maxwell, J. (1999). *The 21 Indispensable Qualities of a Leader: Becoming the Person Others Will Want to Follow.* Nashville, Tenn.: Maxwell Motivational.

Maxwell, J. (2001a). *Developing the Leader within You Workbook.* Nashville, Tenn.: Injoy.

McGraw, P. (2001). *Self Matters: Creating Your Life from the Inside Out.* New York: Free Press.

Wheatly, M. (2002). *Turning to One Another: Simple Conversations to Restore Hope to the Future.* San Francisco: Berrett-Koehler.

3

CREATING A SHARED VISION AND MISSION: PAINTING A PORTRAIT

I dream of painting and then I paint my dreams.

—Vincent van Gogh

LEADERSHIP QUALITIES: COURAGE, INSPIRATION, AND HOPE

Guiding Questions

What is your personal mission and vision?
How do you develop, articulate, and inspire a shared vision? Mission?
How do you enact your mission and vision as a school leader?

Transformational Leadership Fitness Areas

1 Provides a shared vision and goals
3 Fosters commitment
6 Creates high expectations.

SIGHTS TO SEE

Chapter 3 will identify vision and mission as one of the most critical essentials for leadership and organizational success. An effective leader must be able to paint a self-portrait of leadership that begins with a personal mission, vision, and goals for the future. The effective leader is equally responsible to help shape the mission, goals, and vision of a school community. While the self-portrait is completed by the leader alone, the school portrait must be painted by many artists and include multiple perspectives, beliefs, and values. Unlike an abstract painting, valued for its diverse meanings and interpretations, the vision and mission of an organization must be painted with agreed-upon meaning and value. A vision is collaboratively painted that incorporates the ideals and potential of what a community could become. The primary colors in this painting include the beliefs, values, and mission that describe each member of the organization. The vision, therefore, serves as a clear and agreed-upon visual depiction of the promises and commitments the members make to themselves and the organization.

An understanding of words like *mission, vision,* and *goals* is fundamental for leaders in creating a self-portrait. By understanding who they are as leaders they can eventually influence and inspire others. Words like *mission, vision,* and *goals* are used extensively; however, these terms are often more rhetoric than reality. We encourage you to incorporate your personal and organizational vision and mission into your fitness plan. This chapter will define leadership mission and vision on a personal level, and secondly, on an organizational level.

As your guides we will provide you with insights to understand and reflect upon your own mission and vision as a leader. Our approach is also designed to help each leader determine a clear purpose and process in the development of a shared organizational vision and mission. We will provide you with leadership activities, experiences, and examples to assist you in painting a personal and organizational vision and mission.

DEFINING MISSION AND VISION

Creating clear definitions is the first step to creating a shared mission and vision. The leadership literature provides a wide variety of vision and mission definitions. "There is no more powerful engine driving an organization toward excellence and long-range success than an attractive, worthwhile, and achievable vision of the future, widely shared" (Nanus 1992, 3).

This chapter includes generally agreed-upon definitions for "vision," "mission," and "goals." A *vision* is the most abstract of these leadership terms and definitions. Among the dreams, hopes, and ideals of each leader is a vision, the ultimate picture of ideal conditions and potential for the future. *Mission* is our purpose; it is a tangible and achievable gauge of what we will accomplish. Our mission helps us to move from the realistic to the ideal. *Goals* are the steps that help us to achieve our mission. These are specific, measurable, and time bound. Leaders should ask themselves three questions in their efforts to define a mission and vision. Vision: Where are we going? Mission: Why are we here? Goals: What do we have to do to achieve our mission? As leaders we must determine our ideal destination, mission, and goals, first for ourselves and then for our organization.

In any organization, people are asked to contribute pieces to the shared vision. Much like the construction of a puzzle, each piece adds to the clarification of the vision. However, rarely do organizations have the benefit of viewing the "box cover" in order to see the big picture of what these combined pieces can create (Senge, Kleiner, Roberts, Ross, & Smith, 1994).

Creating a Personal Mission

Identifying a personal mission begins when leaders realize and articulate their purpose. Laurie Beth Jones (1998), author of *The Path,* suggests the following elements are needed for an effective mission statement: that it be large enough to encompass a lifetime of activities; that it be summary of your qualities, values, and purpose; and that it be expressible as a clear and concise statement that can be understood by a ten-year-old. A personal mission is stated in terms that are measurable and attainable.

Laurie Beth Jones is one of numerous authors who have tried to identify processes for creating mission statements. As a leader consider your primary purpose, what gets you out of bed in the morning. A mission is a clear and compelling statement that summarizes our purpose. What three action words would describe you and what you want to achieve? My mission is to:

1. _____

2. _____

3. _____

Next, consider your core values and virtues. Some examples are excellence, justice, equality, service, and freedom. What are your primary values?

_____

_____

_____

Thirdly, identify in your mission whom you serve. Examples include children, the elderly, educators, and the community. For example, *My mission is to inspire, empower, and guide* _____ *to make a difference in the lives of children.*

Examples of mission statements:

My mission is to empower teachers to become instructional leaders by providing an environment that encourages reflective practice and collegial networking that is supported by research on best practice.

—High School Department Chair

My mission is to enlarge the lives of others, to create an environment where children and those that serve them will thrive emotionally, intellectually, and socially.

—Educational Leadership Candidate

My mission is to encourage, challenge, and inspire lifelong learning in an honest, fair, and respectful culture that recognizes diversity and benefits our school community.

—Middle School Team Leader

My mission is to create a learning environment for students centered on the principles of honesty, integrity, and excellence that instill in them, through personal example, the values of lifelong learning.

—Educational Leadership Candidate

My mission is to make a difference in each child's educational journey by helping them recognize the positive, productive, and valuable contributions they can make to society.

—Elementary Lead Teacher

We invite you to write your personal mission statement here:

_____

_____

_____

Creating a Personal Vision

Creating our personal vision requires us to be passionate about the future we desire to achieve. This passion should empower us to establish a clear foundation for our purpose and beliefs. The purpose of a personal vision is to think and act in a way that is foresighted, to make a commitment to shape the future, and to build a bridge for change between the present and the future. We need to be clear about our personal vision in order to effectively share it with others. By reflecting further on our leadership experiences, beliefs, mission, and goals, we are able to create our ideal vision of the future.

A paradox exists for some leaders between the development of a personal mission and vision. This mirrors the "chicken or egg" adage. For some leaders it becomes evident that their personal mission will allow them to envision the picture of the ideal. Still others would indicate the importance of establishing an ideal vision before identifying a purpose or mission. In either case, each leader must determine the means that are best suited to establishing a personal vision. Fundamental questions to answer in this process include, What is it that I want to accomplish in the long term? What actions am I prepared to take on a daily basis to support and sustain my vision? What changes am I prepared to make to achieve my vision? How will my mission and beliefs support the vision?

_____

_____

_____

Examples of personal vision statements:

My vision is to create an environment where children can feel safe to learn, where all members find their work satisfying and fulfilling, and where parents feel respected as collaborators in providing the education that will enable children to reach their potential.

—Technology Specialist

My vision is a school that encourages and fosters a caring environment where students, teachers, and administrators interact daily; respects diversity; and is successful in its endeavors.

—Educational Leadership Candidate

My vision of the school is of a place where administrators facilitate positive change and are leaders, and also servants, to the school community, producing a satisfying atmosphere that continually advances all stakeholders to the next level of personal achievement.

—Elementary Lead Teacher

My vision is to create a safe, nurturing environment where students' individual needs are met so as to ensure their academic success by a collaboration of effective leadership, teachers, and community members.

—High School Teacher

What is your personal vision?

_____

_____

_____

CREATING OUR PERSONAL GOALS FOR OUR ACTIONS

Goals assist us in achieving our mission and vision. Actions comprise the day-to-day performance that enables us to reach our goals. One of the most basic exercises in creating a mission and vision is to establish goals. Goal setting is needed at multiple levels, such as individual, team, and organization. A process commonly used to establish goals at all levels of the organization is SMART, a template for goal setting that describes goals as *s*pecific, *m*easurable, *a*ttainable, *r*esults oriented, and *t*ime bound. This method encourages people to think about results that they wish to achieve. When they write goals using this formula, they are more likely to achieve a personal vision and mission. *I will improve* _____ (specific, measurable item) *by* _____ (how much—an attainable amount) *by* _____ (when).

List three of your personal goals as they relate to your mission:

1. _____

2. _____

3. _____

Once we determine our purpose, our fundamental reason for why we are here, we establish goals and a plan to achieve our mission. The goals are the specific steps we will take to achieve our mission, and our actions need to be designed to ensure goal attainment. Like our leadership fitness plan, the actions or exercises that we do every day enable us to achieve our goals. Successful leaders are very deliberate about the actions they take each day, to ensure that they will contribute to their goals. Leaders accomplish this by writing and posting their goals, articulating them with colleagues, and reflecting on them regularly. Reflect upon your beliefs, mission, and goals. Think about how you carry out and act on your goals. How do your actions support your goals and your mission? Identify three actions you have taken or will take that support your goals and mission.

1. _____

2. _____

3. _____

Look at the Beliefs and Vision Worksheet (Exercise 3.2) at the end of this chapter. Indicate your personal beliefs from chapter 2. Also record your personal vision, mission, and goals.

CREATING AN ORGANIZATIONAL MISSION

An organizational mission, like an individual mission, is a statement of purpose, followed by specific goals to be achieved. A mission is a brief, proactive, and compelling statement that serves to unify an organization's efforts. An effective mission must stretch and challenge the organization, yet be achievable. It is tangible, value driven, and highly focused so as to move the organization forward. An effective mission reaches out and grabs people in the gut. It is crisp, clear, and engaging. People get it right away, with little or no explanation.

A school mission can help define a school's purpose; it can be generated by considering some of the cultural features of a school community. First, and most essential, is to determine the existing purpose for the school and its members. This may be illustrated by the values of the teachers, their teaching behaviors, their best practices, and their interactions with others. It is likely that within the school culture some individuals act on the school mission. These individuals generate action and energy that contribute to the achievements of the school community. However, the school leader recognizes the need for a mission and vision to be shared and systematic rather than isolated and individualized.

A leader can help to create a school mission and vision in a variety of approaches. In some cases, it may begin with the desire to define a mission from the existing school culture and build upon it. Another approach may be that the transformational leader would foster support and commitments from the members of the organization to build a shared school mission. In the case of a new school environment, a leader must advocate for the development of both the culture and the school mission by identifying shared values and beliefs.

The process of organizational vision development centers on creating a shared picture of the ideal. Imagine what the behaviors would look like for teachers, students, parents, and administrators on a specific day in the ideal school. Which of these behaviors already exist? What new behaviors could be developed that would contribute to the present or future mission of the school? You will find this as an activity at the end of this chapter (Exercise 3.1).

Examples of organizational missions:

We are committed to providing our employees a stable work environment with equal opportunity for learning and personal growth. Creativity and innovation are encouraged for improving the effectiveness of Southwest Airlines. Above all, employees will be provided the same concern, respect, and caring attitude within the organization that they are expected to share externally with every Southwest customer.

—Southwest Airlines

The entire district community will prepare all students to become lifelong learners who are productive, responsible members of a global society.

—Elementary School District

Our mission is to educate students to be self-directed learners, collaborative workers, complex thinkers, quality producers, and community contributors.

—Unit School District

The mission is to provide and maintain an educational environment where all students succeed, enjoy participating in the school community, establish goals, and leave prepared to reach those goals.

—High School District

CREATING AN ORGANIZATIONAL VISION

The transformational leader facilitates and articulates the school vision as a collaborative effort. It is the school leader who generates the time, energy, and importance to dream. Often these dreams become the organizational vision, ideals that inspire greater standards of excellence. However, these ideals cannot be the dreams of one person. Empowering others to share in building the vision also builds leadership capacity.

Every organization needs more leadership capacity. It is the responsibility of the leader to inspire and influence others toward a shared vision. Often members of an organization vary greatly in their levels of development and understanding of vision. John Maxwell (1993, 141) suggests that vision develops in a variety of ways and at different levels. Some people may be "wanderers" and never see the vision. The "followers" see the vision but never pursue it on their own. "Achievers," however, see the vision and pursue it. Finally, and most importantly, there are "leaders"—people who see the vision, pursue it, and help others to see it. The process of creating a shared vision is highly idiosyncratic and requires leaders to be knowledgeable, committed, and collaborative.

Elaine Wilmore, in her book *Principal Leadership* (2002), recommends four steps for the organizational development of a vision: *development, articulation, implementation,* and *stewardship.*

Vision Development

The first step in creating an organizational vision is to clearly develop the vision, or *destination,* and decide who will make a commitment to travel to this destination. Initially this is accomplished by inviting committed members of the school community to travel together toward a shared dream. During the vision development phase all the stakeholders are included in discussions, collaborations, and decision making. A team then begins to define the ideal organization and what it will take to get there. Exercises to develop an organizational vision are included at the end of this chapter.

Vision Articulation

Next, Wilmore suggests the articulation of a plan for how this vision or destination will be reached. How will we get there? How will we travel? What will it take to get there? What training and fitness will be necessary to begin to carry out a plan for the vision? This step might be articulated at a faculty meeting where members describe an ideal school day or learning environment. It would be likely that parents, students, staff members, and administrators would describe these ideals differently. The articulating of these combined ideals becomes the foundation of the vision.

A community of learners dedicated to preparing informed, involved, principled. and productive citizens and leaders over a lifetime.

—University

Building a passion for life-long learning.

—Unit School District

To build a resourceful bridge between the school and community to help provide a safe, respected, and nationally competitive education to help young individuals be productive in our challenging world.

—Leadership Candidate

Our district strives to maximize the academic, social, and emotional potential of each student by utilizing world class educational practices in partnership with parents, staff, and community.

—Suburban School District

CREATING ORGANIZATIONAL GOALS/ACTIONS

Vision Implementation

The third step of developing a vision, according to Wilmore, is implementation. Now that the destination is clear, members have made a commitment to the vision, and a plan has been established, it is time to put the plan into action. Everyone must be invited to participate in the details of achieving the vision. Once the ideals of the vision have been articulated, members will create goals and strategies that generate an organizational action plan. This action plan represents the organization's promises and obligations to the vision. Each member of the organization becomes responsible to implement and carry out the action plan. The action plan defines the direction the organization's members will follow to move toward the vision.

Vision Stewardship

Step four, according to Wilmore, is often overlooked but is the most critical of all. Sustaining the vision requires a stewardship from those who have created the organization's promises. Once a vision is established, who will safeguard it? Who will sustain the momentum when the others get tired or lose sight of the ideal? The leader is the keeper of the vision and caretaker of those who travel toward the vision. We sustain our vision by constantly articulating, demonstrating, and modeling it, placing it at the forefront of all that we do. It is not enough to make promises for the vision. We must also be an advocate and a voice sustaining our vision to ensure the success of all learners.

Why is the vision and mission one of the essentials of collaborative leadership? A clear mission motivates and energizes people toward a shared purpose. The mission gives direction for the actions, goals, and decisions of the organization and its members.

At the foundation of every organizational mission is a dream and a vision of what the organization can be in the future. With the hope of each generation of children, there must also be hope that the organization will elevate its expectations and achievements. A courageous school leader can inspire and elevate this hope in others.

LEADERSHIP IN ACTION

"As leaders are we only willing to show our right hand? Are we only willing to show our left hand? Or are we willing to show both and reach out with open hands to learn and grow?" Dr. Brian Ali (personal communication, March 3, 2003) is a school superintendent who has reached out with open hands to foster a school community of learning and collaboration. Dr. Ali has attempted to facilitate a shared vision in order to increase the capacity and commitments of the members of the organization. This leadership has helped to transform a school community into a "lighthouse" for learning.

A vision for this district as a lighthouse for others was articulated based on Dr. Ali's own fundamental beliefs: All children can learn, all children deserve the best educators possible in their lives, and as educators, we create the environment that fosters learning. District goals, particularly its numerous attempts to pass a building referendum, evidenced a vision shared between the community and the board of education. In preparation for a third referendum vote, Dr. Ali declared, "This referendum has been a journey, a vision to provide the educational environments critical for student learning. Education opens doors. It is the key to success. It is unacceptable to teach children in closets. There are times when we must become outraged, and times when we have to raise our voices louder."

Among his top priorities, Dr. Ali visually models his beliefs: "Visibility is very important in this job. I try to plan my day around chances to be out of my office and into the schools. I try to create a nurturing environment wherever I go—home, the office, and the community—to model for others by the way I treat people the way I want to be treated."

Dr. Ali has demonstrated high expectations through a relentless effort to articulate the need to provide improved learning facilities for the children in his community. "You have to learn to speak to the ear that is open. . . . You try to create opportunities for others. Together we can open many doors where possibilities abound." Efforts by Dr. Ali to communicate to community members the need for excellence through improved learning conditions were a repeated theme in achieving his vision.

Dr. Ali sets high expectations for himself each day through every interaction with school and community members. He deliberately uses every interaction to plant seeds of commitment and empowerment: "Much like a seed that is planted in the earth, in the dark, you can't see it . . . but the next thing you know is it grows and evolves to a plant . . . much like educating a child. . . . We never know which child in our classroom will be the next one to grow and develop to their greatest potential."

Dr. Ali, as a transformational leader, illustrates the vital role of the school superintendent in building relationships and collaboration among the members of the organization. These relationships were deliberately encouraged and enabled by the superintendent in order to create a reproductive synergy where leadership is planted, nurtured, and grown to its fullest potential. The goal of this leader to make children the centerpiece in all decisions began to transform a community where caring and the pursuit of greater learning became a shared vision.

The impact of school leaders like Dr. Brian Ali on a school community can serve as a model for superintendents, principals, teachers, and future school administrators. "I don't allow titles to get in the way of what people can do. Larger than my job title is my title of 'human being' so I try to keep a frame of mind to be able to work with everyone. It means we must be willing to take risks. Certain people will be more drawn to the mission and more willing to take risks. And this mission for children must be greater than anything."

OBSTACLES AND KEYS

The greatest obstacle that leaders face in creating a shared vision and mission is to determine a process that is understood and accepted by all. The vision and mission process needs to be viewed as critical to the success of educating all children. School communities must develop a process in which all stakeholders feel empowered.

Key in the success of an organization is the ability of each leader to create a personal vision and mission. Before we can paint a shared vision for a school community we need to identify our own personal vision. This personal vision will support the creation of a shared vision and mission for the organization.

LEADERSHIP EXERCISES

The following exercises will provide a framework for leaders to create a shared vision for their organization. By using Exercise 2.2 you will further develop a vision, mission, goals, and an action plan. Leaders should continue to search for evidence or artifacts that showcase their individual and organizational vision.

Exercise 3.1   Painting Our Vision: The Ideal Day

Participants will envision what an ideal school day looks like. Participants should be placed in teams that represent an actual or hypothetical group of students, teachers, parents, administrators, or community members.

Part 1. Describe the behaviors you would see in the ideal school on a specific day. Members of each team will list the ideal behaviors of their assigned group on poster paper. The five lists will be posted around the room. One member of each team will share its ideal behaviors with the large group. Each team will be issued a colored marker and use a "carousel" approach to add ideas to each of the posted lists.

Describe the behaviors of the teachers:

_____

_____

Describe the behaviors of the students:

_____

_____

Describe the behaviors of the parents:

_____

_____

Describe the behaviors of the community members:

_____

_____

Describe the behaviors of the administrators:

_____

_____

Part 2. Place a check mark by the behaviors that presently exist in some form in your school. This part can be conducted as a means to confirm that some of the ideal behaviors of the members of the community already exist.

Part 3. Discuss which of the ideals should become the organizational priorities. Provide adequate discussion time to review the lists and examine how the school members could increase or maximize these behaviors. Provide each participant with ten stickers and ask them to place two on each chart to identify the ideal behaviors from each group that will become organizational priorities.

Part 4. Review the behaviors that were suggested as priorities for each group. Determine goals for each priority area that will generate an action plan that represents the group's promises or commitments to achieve the organizational vision.

Part 5. (Optional) To enrich the activity, recruit members of the subgroups to also take part in this activity. For example, invite students to complete the four steps using the same process as above.

Exercise 3.2   Beliefs and Vision Worksheet

Beliefs
My actions as a leader are based on these beliefs:

_____

_____

_____

_____

Vision
My vision for this organization:

_____

_____

_____

_____

Mission
My mission to accomplish my beliefs:

_____

_____

_____

_____

Goals
Measurable goals to accomplish my mission (specific, measurable, attainable, results oriented, and time-bound):

_____

_____

_____

_____

Action
Specific actions to implement my goals:

_____

_____

_____

_____

Exercise 3.3   Artifact

Identify artifacts or evidence of your leadership vision and mission. Locate or create an artifact to place in your leadership journey album. One artifact may simply be a copy of your present vision or mission. Other artifacts school leaders have identified that illustrate their vision are any school documents that articulate the vision or outcomes from either of the leadership exercises found in this chapter. Take a minute to jot down a few of your vision artifacts that will be placed in your journey album.

_____

_____

_____

_____

Exercise 3.4   Reflective Practice

How have you strengthened your vision and mission development? Identify specific examples of how your vision drives the day-to-day activities in your building.

_____

_____

_____

_____

_____

Dear Diary,

One night while I was watching television I came upon my favorite movie, Camelot. As I watched I was inspired by the mission and vision of King Arthur and the Knights of the Round Table. This mystical saga is a story of a place called Camelot, the ideal in peace, justice, and harmony. It was a time of gallant and chivalrous leadership that featured a king, queen, knight, and a magician. In this age of knights, armor, and chivalry, a new mission could be heard, "Might for right." This mission was created to empower and give a voice to all citizens of Camelot. I could see collaborative leadership at its best modeled by King Arthur, Merlin, Lancelot, and the Knights of the Round Table.

The mission of Camelot was attempted but appeared to fall short of the vision. As I watched King Arthur in his despair and defeat, I was struck by the closing scene. This scene featured a little boy who appeared on the battlefield and reminded King Arthur of Camelot's mission "might for right."

I saw in the little boy the voice and hope of the next generation, much like we see in our children today. This classic story was a reminder to me of the qualities needed as we develop a mission and vision for ourselves and others: courage, inspiration, and hope.

Kris

RESOURCES

DuFour, R., & R. Eaker (1998). *Professional Learning Communities at Work: Best Practices for Enhancing Student Achievement.* Bloomington, Ind.: National Education Service.

Jones, L. (1998). *The Path: Creating Your Mission Statement for Work and for Life.* New York: Hyperion.

Kouzes, J., & B. Posner (1995). *The Leadership Challenge.* San Francisco: Jossey-Bass.

Maxwell, J. (1993). *Developing the Leader within You.* Nashville, Tenn.: Injoy.

Mission Statement Builder. *Franklin Covey.* Retrieved September 21, 2004, from www.franklincovey.com.

Nanus, B. (1992). *Visionary Leadership.* San Francisco: Jossey-Bass.

Robbins, P., & H. Alvy (1995). *The Principal's Companion: Strategies and Hints to Make the Job Easier.* Thousand Oaks, Calif.: Corwin.

Senge, P., A. Kleiner, C. Roberts, R. Ross, & B. Smith (1994). *The Fifth Discipline Fieldbook: Strategies and Tools for Building a Learning Organization.* New York: Doubleday.

Wilmore, E. (2002). *Principal Leadership: Applying the New Educational Leadership Constituent Council (ELCC) Standards.* Thousand Oaks, Calif.: Corwin.

4

LEADERSHIP STANDARDS: A LEADER'S ROAD MAP

Go forth and make a difference in the future of our society—one student and school at a time . . . through the standards you can make a difference.

—Wilmore 2000, 118

LEADERSHIP QUALITIES: VISIONARY, CREATIVE, AND DISCERNMENT

Guiding Questions

What are the leadership standards, and how do they impact a learning community?
Who can benefit by using the leadership standards?
How can leadership standards be used to identify, develop, and assess best practices in leadership?

Transformational Leadership Fitness Areas

2 Models behavior and best practices
5 Provides intellectual stimulation for professional growth
6 Establishes high performance expectations

SIGHTS TO SEE

Standards act as a road map for school leaders. Much like distinctive landmarks on a map, leadership standards serve as conceptual landmarks for leadership development and performance. This chapter will guide leaders to identify, demonstrate, and assess leadership through the use of standards. The leadership standards set a common expectation of knowledge, attitudes, and competencies for aspiring and practicing school leaders. In order for standards to be meaningful, the members of a school community must have a common knowledge and understanding of what constitutes effective leadership. When this exists, transformational leaders are able to establish high expectations, promote and model best practices, and provide support for professional growth.

Ultimately, the greatest measure of successful leadership is its impact on learning. "Best practices" has traditionally been used to identify the top instructional and pedagogical classroom approaches for learning. This chapter will explore the ways in which leadership standards can be used to develop and assess best practices in leading and learning. The standards will provide a framework for leaders to measure and assess their own developmental leadership fitness. "Leadership in Action" will allow you as the leader to identify, demonstrate, and assess your own leadership fitness by utilizing the standards.

WHAT ARE THE LEADERSHIP STANDARDS?

Educational leadership standards have evolved from a variety of sources and organizations. The National Policy Board for Educational Administration (NPBEA), founded in 1988, began to implement standards for such professional organizations as the National Association of Elementary School Principals (NAESP), the National Association of Secondary School Principals (NASSP), and the National Council of Professors of Educational Administration (NCPEA). In 1993 the work of the National Council for Accreditation of Teacher Education (NCATE), National Policy Board for Educational Administration (NPBEA), and the Council of Chief State School Officers (CCSSO) was instrumental in creating the Interstate School Leaders Licensure Consortium (ISLLC), which resulted in the development of the ISLLC standards. The adoption of these standards provided a foundation for all formal leadership positions based on the design of Interstate New Teachers Assessment and Support Consortium (INTASC). The INTASC framework contributed to the use of knowledge, dispositions, and performance to produce a consistent measurement of effective leadership. The joint work of these organizations established a set of six comprehensive standards designed to guide the development and assessment of school leaders. The six standards and 182 indicators of knowledge, dispositions, and competencies were adopted by thirty-five states, as well as NCATE, for educational administration program accreditation.

Educational administrative programs have utilized standards to train and prepare aspiring school leaders. The Educational Leadership Constituent Council (ELCC) collaborated with the American Association of School Administrators (AASA), ISLLC, and NCATE to unify the standards suited for superintendents, principals, and central office staff. The ELCC includes a seventh standard emphasizing the administrative internship for the professional development of leadership candidates.

Educational leadership preparation programs favor the ELCC standards, since they were designed to assess the quality of graduates and programs that prepare future school administrators. Many states have adopted the ISLLC standards as a means to recertify practicing school leaders. In still other cases, organizations have adopted leadership standards to assess school administrators and effective instructional leadership.

School reform, policy changes, and educational accountability explain the increased focus on standards. Efforts to respond to expectations for accreditation from NCATE and NPBEA require standards as a means to develop and assess professional training programs for teachers and administrators. School leaders continue to view standards as a critical centerpiece in the preparation and assessment of school leaders.

Standards as a Concept to Identify Best Practices in Leadership

Standards provide a conceptual target to identify best practices in leadership. Successful leaders desire to demonstrate the best practices of leadership through their beliefs, actions, and performance. However, expectations for high-performance leadership are often ambiguous and idiosyncratic. It is unlikely that individual leaders would identify, develop, or assess effective leadership in the same ways. Without a shared definition of effective leadership, it becomes equally challenging for a second evaluator, such as a superintendent or principal, to assess leadership performance. Douglas Reeves (2004) indicates the organizational implication of an absence of leadership measures and feedback: "The fundamental purpose of leadership evaluation is the improvement of teaching and learning through the building of knowledge and skills of current and prospective educational leaders" (16).

The leadership standards are designed to provide leaders with a comprehensive and philosophical concept of effective leadership. The ISLLC standards state each of six concepts, with students at the core of what effective leaders do. Each of the ISLLC leadership standards begins with a statement promoting student learning and success: "The competent school administrator is an educational leader who promotes the success of all students" (Wilmore 2002, 19). While the standards provide a conceptual framework for leaders, the indicators detail the application of knowledge, dispositions, and actions that leaders need to take to be successful. These will be described as exercises in the following segments of this chapter.

Thomas Sergiovanni (2001) provides a visual approach using the *head, heart,* and *hand* to understand and develop leadership. We will provide you with a framework for understanding and implementing the standards, by merging the standards with Sergiovanni's model. This framework will connect the ISLLC leadership competencies of knowledge, attitudes, and performance, with the head, heart, and hand of leadership.

Sergiovanni (2001) suggests that there are three personal dimensions of leadership, symbolized respectively by the head, the heart, and the hand. The head symbolizes the knowledge and intellectual side of successful leadership. Leaders develop knowledge through educational leadership programs, professional development, conferences, professional literature, and collegial relationships. The heart, the second leadership image in this model, represents the beliefs and values of leaders. "The heart of leadership has to do with what a person believes, values, dreams about, and is committed to—that person's personal vision" (Sergiovanni 2001, 343). Likewise, the second level of the leadership standards addresses the dispositions and attitudes of effective leaders. Through reflective practice, like the "Raising the BAR" activity in chapter 2, leaders become more aware of the beliefs that guide their actions. In this model the heart is often the emotional and affective side of leadership.

The last symbol of leadership, the hand, represents the decisions and performance of leaders. These are the strategies, behaviors, and actions leaders demonstrate within the organization. Sergiovanni (2001) suggests the hand, as well as the heart and head, comprises "personal reflections not only of our vision and practical theories but our personalities and our responses to the unique situations we face" (308). A leader's performance is inevitably guided by the first two areas of knowledge and beliefs. When the head, heart, and hand are congruent, leadership practices rise to the highest level.

Standards as a Tool to Develop Leadership

The standards provide a conceptual framework for understanding, while the indicators become a tool for implementation and performance. As a tool, the indicators provide leaders with benchmarks to take action and strengthen performance. The application of standards is useful for those in the initial development of leadership certification and the continued implementation and development of practicing leaders, and for those who aspire to future leadership positions.

The standards are increasingly used as an instrument in leadership programs to teach and assess leadership candidates seeking administrative certification. The addition of a seventh standard for internship experiences by leadership candidates was proposed by the NCATE and the ELCC: "A school administrator is an educational leader who promotes the success of all students through substantial, sustained, standards-based experiences in real settings that are planned and guided cooperatively by university and school district personal for graduate credit" (Wilmore 2002, 103). Prospective leaders can experience long-term professional benefits by connecting the standards with internships in authentic school environments. However, many educational leadership preparation programs provide only limited internship or practical fieldwork opportunities. The beginning principal, therefore, enters the challenges of a first job with limited or no practical field experience, little mentoring or guidance, and a minimal understanding of the standards. The standards also become a critical tool for the beginning administrator as a self-guide for leadership enhancement. Unfortunately, many practicing school leaders today have experienced neither the standards nor adequate internships.

The use of standards for active leaders has different benefits from those learning in a formal administrative leadership program. Doug Reeves, for his book *Assessing Educational Leaders* (2004), conducted extensive surveys and compiled documents of experiences and evaluations of leaders. He suggests that evaluation systems, while critical for improvement and accountability of leaders, are deeply flawed: "These systems fail to recognize excellence, give encouragement to bad practice, tolerate mediocrity, turn a blind eye to abusive practice, accept incompetence, and systematically demoralize courageous and committed leaders" (2). These conditions sound grim, but efforts to improve leadership through evaluation and the implementation of standards are under way. This book and many others take the optimistic view that leadership performance is making progress through standards. This progress begins when individual leaders become aware of the standards and utilize the indicators as tools for developing skills and performance.

Three methods are provided in this chapter for practicing leaders to utilize the standards as a tool for improving performance. First, leaders must acquire an understanding of the standards and their existing level of knowledge, attitudes, and performance. Through a self-assessment, which is featured in this chapter, each leader will use the leadership standards to determine areas of competence and areas that need improvement.

A second critical area of leadership development and improvement is the formulation of exercises to improve targeted skills. For example, a middle school leader may experience a low score for the development of appropriate adolescent instructional practices. The indicator states, "The competent leader applies principles of student development to the learning environment and educational program." What action or exercises would you develop to improve instructional awareness of adolescent development?

_____

_____

_____

Additional examples will be provided in the "Leadership in Action" section.

Building leadership capacity is a third area in which the standards can be used as a tool for leadership development. The standards provide lead teachers with a preview of and means to begin to practice the attitudes and skills required for increased leadership contributions. The leadership standards, when utilized with aspiring leaders, can increase future leadership capacity within the organization.

Standards as a Measurement of Leadership

In order to improve performance there must be a means to measure it. The role of school leaders has traditionally lacked standardized measures. The standards serve as both informal and formal templates for measuring the performance of leaders. An important point to consider is the *knowing/ doing gap* that has been described between what leaders know and how they behave: "This gap provides clear evidence that the evaluation systems that are now in place display an intellectual understanding of what needs to be done, but lack the fundamental ability to act on that knowledge" (Reeves 2004, 3). Leaders consistently demonstrate a gap between knowledge of high performance leadership skills and the ability to demonstrate them.

The leadership standards provide a framework by which leaders can act upon the knowledge of how successful leaders perform. "Leadership in Action" will ask you to complete a self-assessment of the ISLLC leadership standards. You will rate your competencies on a scale of five to one, identifying your leadership strengths and areas for improvement. The exercises at the end of this chapter include a "Leadership Fitness Inventory" (Exercise 4.1) as a summary of your leadership competencies.

The "Leadership Fitness Inventory" will allow the leader to assess and put into practice what is known about effective leadership. This begins with how leader might use the results of the inventory. One method is to use the individual results and determine specific exercises to improve as a leader. This becomes your leadership fitness plan. Another alternative would be to invite a colleague or team to complete the assessment as well; the participants would share results and suggestions with one another on ways to improve. Who would you be willing to invite to complete and share the results of your inventory?

_____

What team or committee would benefit from completing the "Leadership in Action" section?

_____

_____

A leadership fitness plan can be designed by identifying goals as a result of the leadership inventory. Consider utilizing the SMART goals strategy that was provided in chapter 3. How will you determine evidence of improvement for each of these goals? Examples will be provided in the third exercise at the end of this chapter. Finally, once leadership is initially developed, it must be sustained. Consider once again leadership as a fitness model. The standards' indicators are exercises that develop over time and improve with practice. Given time and a genuine commitment, leaders will further strengthen and improve their leadership fitness. However, as in a physical-fitness workout program, leaders must set clear goals, create exercises to achieve the goals, and measure improvement.

LEADERSHIP IN ACTION

The following self-assessment can be used for all levels and positions of leadership. It has been aligned as a framework that illustrates the ISLLC standards and Sergiovanni's (2001) model of the head, heart, and hand. Assign a proficiency rating of five to one for each of the leadership standards and competencies. After you have completed the assessment, note the strength areas—those in which you have scored a four or five. Equally important, what areas have you given a score of two or three, indicating a need for further development? Consider your leadership style as it relates to the model of the heart, head, and hand. What areas are your strengths? In what areas will you need to exercise new or undeveloped leadership skills? This assessment will be a significant and rigorous exercise for the transformational leader.

Leadership Standards: Self-Assessment

5 = Highly Proficient; 4 = Proficient; 3 = Progressing; 2 = Limited Proficiency; 1 = Little or No Proficiency

---

STANDARD 1

A school administrator is an educational leader who promotes the success of all students by facilitating the development, articulation, implementation, and stewardship of a vision of learning that is shared and supported by the school community.

Knowledge

The administrator has knowledge and understanding of:

_____ the principles of developing and implementing strategic plans (1A)
_____ theories of educational leadership (1B)
_____ information sources, data collection, and data analysis strategies (1C)
_____ effective communication (1D)
_____ effective consensus-building and negotiation skills (1E)

Attitudes

The administrator believes in, values, and is committed to:

_____ the educability of all (1F)
_____ a school vision of high standards of learning (1G)
_____ continuous school improvement (1H)
_____ the inclusion of all members of the school community (1I)
_____ ensuring that students have the knowledge, skills, and values needed to become successful adults (1J)

_____ a willingness to continuously examine one's own assumptions, beliefs, and practices (1K)

_____ doing the work required for high levels of personal and organization performance (1L).

Performance

The administrator facilitates processes and engages in activities ensuring that:

_____ the vision and mission of the school are effectively communicated to staff, parents, students, and community members (1M)

_____ the vision and mission are communicated through the use of symbols, ceremonies, stories, and similar activities (1N)

_____ the core beliefs of the school vision are modeled for all stakeholders (1O)

_____ the vision is developed with and among stakeholders (1P)

_____ the contributions of school community members to the realization of the vision are recognized and celebrated (1Q)

_____ progress toward the vision and mission is communicated to all stakeholders (1R)

_____ the school community is involved in school-improvement efforts (1S)

_____ the vision shapes the educational programs, plans, and actions (1T)

_____ an implementation plan is developed in which objectives and strategies to achieve the vision and goals are clearly articulated (1U)

_____ assessment data related to student learning are used to develop the school vision and goals (1V)

_____ relevant demographic data pertaining to students and their families are used in developing the school mission and goals (1W)

_____ barriers to achieving the vision are identified, clarified, and addressed (1X)

_____ needed resources are sought and obtained to support the implementation of the school mission and goals (1Y)

_____ existing resources are used in support of the school vision and goals (1Z)

_____ the vision, mission, and implementation plans are regularly monitored, evaluated, and revised (1AA)

Reflective Practice

What is your vision of the ideal school? What will it take to get there? Who else will share and help to build this vision?

_____

_____

_____

_____

_____

Select three to five indicators that might be considered areas of priority for your school, team, or department.

1. _____
2. _____
3. _____
4. _____
5. _____

STANDARD 2

A school administrator is an educational leader who promotes the success of all students by advocating, nurturing, and sustaining a school culture and instructional program conducive to student learning and staff professional growth.

Knowledge

The administrator has knowledge and understanding of:

_____ student growth and development (2A)
_____ applied learning theories (2B)
_____ applied motivational theories (2C)
_____ curriculum design, implementation, evaluation, and refinement (2D)
_____ principles of effective instruction (2E)
_____ measurement, evaluation, and assessment strategies (2F)
_____ diversity and its meaning for educational programs (2G)
_____ adult learning and professional development models (2H)
_____ the change process for systems, organizations, and individuals (2I)
_____ the role of technology in promoting student learning and professional growth (2J)
_____ school culture (2K)

Attitudes

The administrator believes in, values, and is committed to:

_____ student learning as the fundamental purpose of schooling (2L)
_____ the proposition that all students can learn (2M)
_____ the variety of ways in which students can learn (2N)
_____ lifelong learning for self and others (2O)
_____ professional development as an integral part of school improvement (2P)
_____ the benefits that diversity brings to the school community (2Q)

_____ a safe and supportive learning environment (2R)

_____ preparing students to be contributing members of society (2S)

Performance

The administrator facilitates processes and engages in activities ensuring that:

_____ all individuals are treated with fairness, dignity, and respect (2T)

_____ professional development promotes a focus on student learning consistent with the school vision and goals (2U)

_____ students and staff feel valued and important (2V)

_____ the responsibilities and contributions of each individual are acknowledged (2W)

_____ barriers to student learning are identified, clarified, and addressed (2X)

_____ diversity is considered in developing learning experiences (2Y)

_____ lifelong learning is encouraged and modeled (2Z)

_____ there is a culture of high expectations for self, student, and staff performance (2AA)

_____ technologies are used in teaching and learning (2BB)

_____ student and staff accomplishments are recognized and celebrated (2CC)

_____ multiple opportunities to learn are available to all students (2DD)

_____ the school is organized and aligned for success (2EE)

_____ curricular, cocurricular, and extracurricular programs are designed, implemented, evaluated, and refined (2FF)

_____ curriculum decisions are based on research, expertise of teachers, and the recommendations of learned societies (2GG)

_____ the school culture and climate are assessed on a regular basis (2HH)

_____ a variety of sources of information are used to make decisions (2II)

_____ student learning is assessed using a variety of techniques (2JJ)

_____ multiple sources of information regarding performance are used by staff and students (2KK)

_____ a variety of supervisory and evaluation models are employed (2LL)

_____ pupil programs are developed to meet the needs of students and their families (2MM)

Reflective Practice

Identify evidence that represents your school culture. Consider these areas: What is the school history? What are significant past events? What ceremonies or rituals receive the most attention? What symbols are used?

_____

_____

_____

_____

_____

Identify your school improvement goals and how your learning culture will support achieving these goals.

_____

_____

_____

_____

_____

STANDARD 3

A school administrator is an educational leader who promotes the success of all students by ensuring management of the organization, operations, and resources for a safe, efficient, and effective learning environment.

Knowledge

The administrator has knowledge and understanding of:

_____ theories and models of organizations and the principles of organizational development (3A)

_____ operational procedures at the school and district levels (3B)

_____ principles and issues relating to school safety and security (3C)

_____ human resources management and development (3D)

_____ principles and issues relating to fiscal operations of school management (3E)

_____ principles and issues relating to school facilities and use of space (3F)

_____ legal issues impacting school operations (3G)

_____ current technologies that support management functions (3H)

Attitudes

The administrator believes in, values, and is committed to:

_____ making management decisions to enhance learning and teaching (3I)

_____ taking risks to improve schools (3J)

_____ trusting people and their judgments (3K)

_____ accepting responsibility (3L)

_____ high-quality standards, expectations, and performances (3M)

_____ involving stakeholders in management processes (3N)

_____ a safe environment (3O)

Performance

The administrator facilitates processes and engages in activities ensuring that:

_____ knowledge of learning, teaching, and student development is used to inform management decisions (3P)

_____ operational procedures are designed and managed to maximize opportunities for successful learning (3Q)

_____ emerging trends are recognized, studied, and applied as appropriate (3R)

_____ operational plans and procedures to achieve the vision and goals of the school are in place (3S)

_____ collective bargaining and other contractual agreements related to the school are effectively managed (3T)

_____ the school plant, equipment, and support systems operate safely, efficiently, and effectively (3U)

_____ time is managed to maximize attainment of organizational goals (3V)

_____ potential problems and opportunities are identified (3W)

_____ problems are confronted and resolved in a timely manner (3X)

_____ financial, human, and material resources are aligned to the goals of school (3Y)

_____ the school acts entrepreneurially to support continuous improvement (3Z)

_____ organizational systems are regularly monitored and modified as needed (3AA)

_____ stakeholders are involved in decisions affecting school (3BB)

_____ responsibility is shared to maximize ownership and accountability (3CC)

_____ effective problem-framing and problem-solving skills are used (3DD)

_____ effective conflict-resolution skills are used (3EE)

_____ effective group-process and consensus-building skills are used (3FF)

_____ effective communication skills are used (3GG)

_____ a safe, clean, and aesthetically pleasing school environment is created and maintained (3HH)

_____ human resource functions support the attainment of school goals (3II)

_____ confidentiality and privacy of school records are maintained (3JJ)

Reflective Practice

Identify examples of how your school provides a safe and effective environment for learning.

_____

_____

_____

_____

_____

_____

Schools require a good balance of leadership and management. Identify five examples of effective management that contribute to your school vision and learning culture.

1. _____

2. _____

3. _____

4. _____

5. _____

STANDARD 4

A school administrator is an educational leader who promotes the success of all students by collaborating with families and community members, responding to diverse community interests and needs, and mobilizing community resources.

Knowledge

The administrator has knowledge and understanding of:

_____ emerging issues and trends that potentially impact the school community (4A)

_____ the conditions and dynamics of the diverse school community (4B)

_____ community resources (4C)

_____ community relations and marketing strategies and processes (4D)

_____ successful models of school, family, business, community, government and higher education partnerships (4E)

Attitudes

The administrator believes in, values, and is committed to:

_____ schools operating as an integral part of the larger community (4F)

_____ collaboration and communication with families (4G)

_____ involvement of families and other stakeholders in school decision-making processes (4H)

_____ the proposition that diversity enriches the school (4I)

_____ families as partners in the education of their children (4J)

_____ the proposition that families have the best interests of their children in mind (4K)

_____ bringing the resources of the family and community to bear on the education of students (4L)

_____ an informed public (4M)

Performance

The administrator facilitates processes and engages in activities ensuring that:

_____ high visibility, active involvement, and communication with the larger community are a priority (4N)

_____ relationships with community leaders are identified and nurtured (4O)

_____ information about family and community concerns, expectations, and needs is used regularly (4P)

_____ there is outreach to different business, religious, political, and service agencies and organizations (4Q)

_____ credence is given to individuals and groups whose values and opinions may conflict (4R)

_____ the school and community serve one another as resources (4S)

_____ available community resources are secured to help the school solve problems and achieve goals (4T)

_____ partnerships are established with area businesses, institutions of higher education, and community groups to strengthen programs and support school goals (4U)

_____ community youth family services are integrated with school programs (4V)

_____ community stakeholders are treated equitably (4W)

_____ diversity is recognized and valued (4X)

_____ effective media relations are developed and maintained (4Y)

_____ a comprehensive program of community relations is established (4Z)

_____ public resources and funds are used appropriately and wisely (4AA)

_____ community collaboration is modeled for staff (4BB)

_____ opportunities for staff to develop collaborative skills are provided (4CC)

Reflective Practice

Identify five artifacts that illustrate collaboration within your school community.

1. _____

2. _____

3. _____

4. _____

5. _____

Identify five examples of partnerships from your school community.

1. _____

2. _____

3. _____

4. _____

5. _____

STANDARD 5

A school administrator is an educational leader who promotes the success of all students by acting with integrity and fairness, and in an ethical manner.

Knowledge

The administrator has knowledge and understanding of:

_____ the purpose of education and the role of leadership in modern society (5A)
_____ various ethical frameworks and perspectives on ethics (5B)
_____ the values of the diverse school community (5C)
_____ professional codes of ethics (5D)
_____ the philosophy and history of education (5E)

Attitudes

The administrator believes in, values, and is committed to:

_____ the ideal of the common good (5F)
_____ the principles of the Bill of Rights (5G)
_____ the right of every student to a free, quality education (5H)
_____ bringing ethical principles to the decision-making process (5I)
_____ subordinating one's own interest to the good of the school community (5J)
_____ accepting the consequences for upholding one's principles and actions (5K)
_____ using the influence of one's office constructively and productively in the service of all students and their families (5L)
_____ the development of a caring school community (5M)

Performance

The administrator:

_____ examines personal and professional values (5N)
_____ demonstrates a personal and professional code of ethics (5O)
_____ demonstrates values, beliefs, and attitudes that inspire others to higher levels of performance (5P)

_____ serves as a role model (5Q)

_____ accepts responsibility for school operations (5R)

_____ considers the impact of one's administrative practices on others (5S)

_____ uses the influence of the office to enhance the educational program rather than for personal gain (5T)

_____ treats people fairly, equitably, and with dignity and respect (5U)

_____ protects the rights and confidentiality of students and staff (5V)

_____ demonstrates appreciation for and sensitivity to the diversity in the school community (5W)

_____ recognizes and respects the legitimate authority of others (5X)

_____ examines that others in the school community will demonstrate integrity and exercise ethical behavior (5Y)

_____ opens the school to public scrutiny (5Z)

_____ fulfills the legal and contractual obligations (5AA)

_____ applies laws and procedures fairly, wisely, and considerately (5BB)

Reflective Practice

Identify three ways that you demonstrate values, beliefs, and attitudes to inspire others to higher levels of performance.

1. _____

2. _____

3. _____

How would you like to improve as a school leader in the areas of integrity and fairness?

_____

_____

_____

STANDARD 6

A school administrator is an educational leader who promotes the success of all students by understanding, responding to, and influencing the larger political, social, economic, legal, and cultural context.

Knowledge

The administrator has knowledge and understanding of:

_____ the role of public education in developing and renewing a democratic society and an economically productive nation (6A)

_____ the law as related to education and schooling (6B)

_____ the political, social, cultural, and economic systems and processes that impact schools (6C)

_____ models and strategies of change and conflict resolution as applied to the larger political, social, cultural, and economic contexts of schooling (6D)

_____ global issues and forces affecting teaching and learning (6E)

_____ the dynamics of policy development and advocacy under our democratic political system (6F)

_____ the importance of diversity and equity in a democratic society (6G)

Attitudes

The administrator believes in, values, and is committed to:

_____ education as a key to opportunity and social mobility (6H)

_____ recognizing a variety of ideas, values, and cultures (6I)

_____ importance of a continuing dialogue with other decision makers affecting education (6J)

_____ actively participating in the political and policy-making context in the service of education (6K)

_____ using legal systems to protect student rights and improve student opportunities (6L)

Performance

The administrator facilitates processes and engages in activities ensuring that:

_____ the environment in which schools operate is influenced on behalf of students and their families (6M)

_____ communication occurs among the school community concerning trends, issues, and potential changes in the environment in which schools operate (6N)

_____ there is ongoing dialogue with representatives of diverse community groups (6O)

_____ the school community works within the framework of policies, laws, and regulations enacted by local, state, and federal authorities (6P)

_____ public policy is shaped to provide quality education for students (6Q)

_____ lines of communication are developed with decision makers outside the school community (6R)

Reflective Practice

Identify one indicator that you would like to improve upon in Standard 6.

_____

OBSTACLES AND KEYS

The greatest obstacle leaders face with leadership standards is failure to utilize them. It would be a failure on the part of a traveler not to utilize a map as an important navigational tool. Leaders who fail to use the standards to understand, develop, and assess leadership similarly risk not reaching their destinations as leaders.

The key to the leadership standards is to individualize them to each leader's role, experience, and skills. For the lead teacher from the classroom, moderate knowledge and limited application would be considered very successful. On the other hand, principals who are responsible for a large staff and student body and a diverse learning community cannot afford to be limited in their knowledge or application. Such leaders must demonstrate their knowledge through actions to meet the unique needs of their organization.

LEADERSHIP EXERCISES

The following exercises will assist you in the growth and development of your leadership skills. You will be asked to identify evidence or artifacts that showcase your leadership performance. You are encouraged to utilize these exercises both individually and collectively within your school community.

Exercise 4.1   Leadership Fitness Inventory

Consider the results of your leadership assessment. Identify the areas in which you had the highest scores. List these areas below under the appropriate standards. List the areas in which you rated yourself with a score that you would like to improve. What does the inventory tell you about your leadership development and competencies?

Standard	Strength Areas	Improvement Areas
Vision		
Culture		
Management		
Partnership		
Ethics		
Politics		

Exercise 4.2   Fitness Exercise Plan

Identify leadership feedback or assessment that has been provided to you. Areas where you might find this would be a performance evaluation, feedback from a supervisor, or your leadership fitness inventory from exercise 4.1. Identify three to five areas in which you would like to most improve. Next, determine the action or exercise you will take to improve this leadership skill. Lastly, determine what evidence or artifacts you would use to measure your improvement.

Leadership Fitness Plan

Leadership Goals	Exercises	Measurement
1. The vision is developed with and among stakeholders (IP)	Invite parents, students, and community members to actively participate on the building leadership team	Provide a survey to building leadership team participants to assess yearly accomplishments
2.		
3.		
4.		

Exercise 4.3 Leadership Standards in Action

TASK 1

Determine a team who will identify evidence or indicators of the leadership standards within your school. Much like an archeologist, you may need to dig to discover some of the most valuable leadership evidence within a school.

TASK 2

Identify, collect, and create a file of as many artifacts as possible for one of the standards. These may be existing artifacts, observed actions or events, or conversations with stakeholders in the school. Review the indicators found in the school leadership standards as examples of what you should look for in each school.

TASK 3

After gathering your artifacts, analyze each one to determine how it represents one or more of the leadership standards. Each participant in this activity will assign a point value for each artifact. Communicate the rationales for the value appointed to each of the artifacts to the other team members.

Standards-Based Artifact Search
Sample

Team: The Cardinals

Standard 1: A school administrator is an educational leader who promotes the success of all students by facilitating the development, articulation, implementation, and stewardship of a vision of learning that is shared and supported by the school community.

Artifact File—Item, Value, and Description:

Artifacts Collected	Value (1–10)	Rationale
✔ Vision statement	5	posted but not enacted
✔ School improvement goals	10	shared ownership by all staff
✔ Student work sample	10	schoolwide writing curriculum
✔ Teacher book study	10	active learning and risk taking
✔ Team leader workshop	7	teacher empowerment
✔ Principal attendance at national conference	10	professional growth
✔ Description of principal by teacher	4	personal insights
✔ Student council governance	7	strong student voice
✔ End-of-the-year celebration	7	positive tradition to recognize success

Exercise 4.4   Artifact

Identify several of the artifacts collected in Exercise 4.3. How are these reflective of your leadership?

_____

_____

_____

_____

Exercise 4.5   Reflective Practice

How can the leadership standards be used to improve best practices in my school?

_____

_____

_____

_____

_____

Dear Diary,

One day while I was out golfing, I realized that the use of leadership standards was a lot like golf. Par on a golf course establishes the expectation of what we are shooting for. The flags and greens provide the target. The tee box provides a choice of difficulty and where we are to begin. The course conditions can vary with the environment, and the white markers give us the boundaries we must play within. The distance markers on the course define our progress. Our golf clubs are the tools by which we reach our goals.

Golfers, like leaders, bring their own ranges of mental and physical preparedness to the game. We have a choice in golf, as in leadership: accept the beauty of your surroundings or see only the challenges. Every hole offers the golfer a fresh start and a new opportunity to set their standards high and work to achieve them.

Kellie

RESOURCES

Fullan, M. (2001). *Leading in a Culture of Change.* San Francisco: Jossey-Bass.

Green, R. L. (2001). *Practicing the Art of Leadership: A Problem-Based Approach to Implementing the ISLLC Standards.* Columbus, Ohio: Prentice Hall.

Interstate Consortium on School Leadership. *Council of Chief State School Officers.* Retrieved September 21, 2005, from www.ccsso.org.

Reeves, D. (2004). *Assessing Educational Leaders: Evaluating Performance for Improved Individual and Organizational Results.* Thousands Oaks, Calif.: Corwin.

Sergiovanni, Thomas J. (2001). *The Principalship: A Reflective Practice Perspective.* 4th edition. Boston: Allyn and Bacon.

Wilmore, E. (2002). *Principal Leadership: Applying the New Educational Leadership Constituent Council (ELCC) Standards.* Thousand Oaks, Calif.: Corwin.

PART 2

THE JOURNEY

5

WE VS. ME: BUILDING SUCCESSFUL TEAMS

Teams, not individuals, are the fundamental learning unit in modern organizations; unless the team can learn, the organization cannot.

—Senge 1990, 10

LEADERSHIP QUALITIES: COLLABORATION, COMMUNICATION, AND ACCOUNTABILITY

Guiding Questions

Why Teaming?
What are the characteristics of high-performance teams?
How do we build and sustain an organizational teaming framework?

Transformational Leadership Fitness Areas

2 Models behavior and best practices
3 Fosters commitment.

SIGHTS TO SEE

Building and sustaining effective organizational teams is the first leg of our leadership journey. This chapter will provide opportunities for leaders to build, strengthen, and sustain teaming and team structures within their learning communities. We have spent the last four chapters preparing for the challenges of leadership, and we hope you feel well prepared for the journey that lies ahead. Most leaders and organizations would readily agree on the significance of teaming for success. It is unlikely that either leaders or organizations can be successful without effective teaming structures.

This chapter will describe ways for organizations to better design, develop, and utilize high-performing teams for high-performance results. Tools will be provided to assist leaders in establishing and sustaining high-performing teams within the organization. This chapter will also provide leaders with a means to align teams within the organization by utilizing a common teaming framework. The "Wizard of Oz Team" will be featured as an example of a high-performance team. This chapter will conclude with "Leadership in Action," which features examples of actual products of and tools utilized by high-performance teams.

WHY TEAMING?

The purpose of teams is to meet the organizational mission, vision, and goals. Teaming is the process and mechanism by which the organization can learn and grow. Successful teams collaborate to achieve individual, team, and organizational goals. "Collaboration is a purposeful relationship in which all parties strategically choose to cooperate in order to accomplish a shared outcome" (Rubin 2002, 17).

Teams are created to achieve specific organizational tasks and goals. Teaming provides opportunities for organizations to reach heights that could not be accomplished by individuals working alone. Teams may be identified as committees, task forces, departments, grade-level teams, community partnerships, boards, councils, home school partnerships, and district leadership teams. Regardless of what teams are called within an organization, they are each created for a defined purpose. In addition to teams having a technical purpose, they also contribute to the socialization and the satisfaction people experience when they work together toward a common goal.

Transformational leaders understand that members must desire to build and sustain relationships in order to achieve team and organizational fitness. The following segments will introduce organizational teaming methods to build and align high-performance teams.

WHAT ARE THE CHARACTERISTICS OF
HIGH-PERFORMANCE TEAMS?

High-performance teams increase the likelihood that team and organizational goals will be achieved. Examples of high-performance teams can be found in a variety of venues, such as sports, business, and education. Think about what these high-performing teams have in common. Describe the behaviors of a high-performing team that you have been associated with.

_____

_____

_____

Describe the behaviors of a low-performing team that you have been associated with.

_____

_____

_____

What were the primary differences between these teams?

_____

_____

_____

A team will be described that characterizes the features of high-performance teams. This fictional team is known by virtually everyone and is a lighthearted example of teaming—the Wizard of Oz team. This team is made up of Dorothy, Toto, Scarecrow, Tin Man, and the Lion. On the journey to the Emerald City, these teammates followed a common path, the Yellow Brick Road. Each brought a diverse strength and played a unique role to support their teammates. Although Dorothy had natural leadership skills, each member played a leadership role during the journey to Oz. Each had a goal that none could meet alone—but that could be met through the support and guidance of the team. They collaborated and supported each member's individual goal, knowing this would help the individual as well as the group to be successful.

The Oz team had many characteristics of a high-performing team. These characteristics included shared decision making, diverse strengths, shared leadership, effective communication, mutual trust and respect, and common goals. The goals for the Oz Team were challenging, but all the members of the team agreed to travel to the same destination.

Identify a goal that you share with a team. How was this goal developed?

_____

_____

_____

HOW CAN WE BUILD AND SUSTAIN HIGH-PERFORMANCE TEAMS?

To build and sustain high-performance teams, organizations need to systematically follow four process steps. The first step to the systematic improvement of teaming is to identify a common framework or model suited to the organizational goals. Next, this framework is comprehensively applied to all teams in order to establish consistent organizational teaming expectations and performance. The third step is to determine teaming tools necessary to strengthen the people, processes, and products of each team. The fourth step requires that once a framework and tools have been established, a mechanism to assess team performance be implemented.

Collaborative organizations use frameworks in order to understand, navigate, and convey meaning to others. Metaphors such as maps, tools, and frames are frequently used in leadership to enhance understanding and provide new perspectives. "As a mental map, a frame is a set of ideas or assumptions you carry in your head. It helps you to understand and negotiate a particular territory. . . . Frames are windows on the world of leadership and management. A good frame makes it easier to know what you are up against and what you can do about it. . . . Like maps, frames are both windows on a territory and tools for navigation" (Bolman & Deal 2003, 12).

Before choosing a framework it is important for leaders to reflect on their own fitness, beliefs, and vision, as discussed in the first three chapters. Once individual leadership fitness has been established, it is vital that the same essentials be developed at the team and organizational level. How would you assess leadership fitness, beliefs, and vision as an individual, team, and organization?

Individual Fitness >>>>>>> Team Fitness >>>>>>> Organizational Fitness
Beliefs >>>>>>>　　　　Beliefs >>>>>>>　　　　　Beliefs
Vision >>>>>>>　　　　　Vision >>>>>>>　　　　　Vision

A teaming framework benefits the organization by: (1) promoting consistency in team performance; (2) providing a uniform way to introduce and utilize teaming tools; and (3) assessing the process, products, and performance of teams. The five frameworks featured in this chapter were selected for the distinct and prominent teaming qualities each provides. Leaders should take into account the culture of the organization when selecting a teaming model. Chapter 6 will provide you with ways to assess your culture and compatible frameworks to enhance teaming. School leaders may wish to select one of the following teaming frameworks or create their own framework using features that are best suited to organizational needs (see table 5.1).

The descriptions that follow provide the reader with a brief background on the strengths of the teaming frameworks. Kenneth Leithwood has conducted extensive research on transformational leadership and offers evidence of the relationship between educational leadership and student achievement. As a model his work offers a practical and powerful approach to collaborative leadership in which all members of the organization contribute to its leadership capacity. *Changing Leadership for Changing Times* (1999) by Leithwood, Jantzi, and Steinbach is a resource for organizations that wish to implement transformational leadership through a schoolwide model to enhance team building.

The Arnold and Stevenson teaming model is frequently used in middle schools and has gained popularity due to its focus on human relationships, clarity, and anecdotes. *Teachers' Teaming Handbook: A Middle Level Planning Guide* (1998), based on eight teaming features, includes extensive

Table 5.1　Teaming Frameworks

Katzenbach and Smith: The Wisdom of Teams	Leithwood, Jantzi, and Steinbach: Transformational Leadership	DuFour and Eaker: Professional Learning Communities	Scholtes: The Team Handbook	Arnold and Stevenson: Teachers' Teaming Handbook
Define purpose	Building a shared vision	Shared vision, mission, and values	Clarity in team goals	Team vision and philosophy
Establish clear goals	Models best practices	Collective inquiry	A growth and improvement plan	Team governance
Manageable team size	Fosters commitment	Collaborative teams	Define beneficial team behaviors	Organization and procedures
The right mix of expertise	Individualized support	Action orientation and experimentation	Roles and responsibilities	Creating identity and recognition
Relationship building	Professional development	Continuous improvement	Clear communication	Communication
	Establishes high expectations		Balanced participation	Curriculum
			Establish ground rules	Accountability
			Awareness of group processes	Teacher Efficacy

principles, scenarios, and guidelines for every conceivable team. This resource should not be limited to middle schools. Middle-school teams, administrative leadership classes, and undergraduate education classes have utilized this teaming text. In figure 5.1 you will find an example of how a team may utilize Stevenson and Arnold's framework.

Scholtes has been well known in teaming for organizations for several decades. *The Team Handbook* (1988) is designed for quality leadership through systematic improvement and scientific, data-based decision making. It is a "how to" book for teams, filled with tools, checklists, and activities. *Ingredients for a Successful Team* is a partial framework taken from the many models offered in Peter Scholtes's comprehensive handbook on teaming.

The Wisdom of Teams (1993) is considered by many to be one of the top resources in teaming. Katzenbach and Smith define teaming as "a small number of people with complementary skills, who are committed to a common purpose, set of performance goals and approach for which they hold themselves mutually accountable" (45). Katzenbach and Smith provide a framework of six distinguishing features of high-performing teams based on extensive interviews and data collection on teaming. Schools and businesses use *The Wisdom of Teams* to systematically organize and develop high-performance teams.

"Professional learning communities" have gained tremendous appeal in schools as a comprehensive framework for school reform. The six broad characteristics described by DuFour and Eaker in *Professional Learning Communities at Work* (1998) reflect the strengths of numerous other models. These frequently begin with an emphasis on vision, mission, and values. Collaborative teams and continuous improvement are also characteristics of this model and are significant in organizational literature. Table 5.2 features a combination of the professional-learning-communities framework, with the seven tools for effective teams that follow; examples are provided.

While one model may meet many organizational needs, an eclectic approach in which some characteristics from different frameworks are combined might offer a more customized model. Take some time to choose a framework from table 5.1 or select a combination of components that you wish to further develop as a teaming model. Identify the primary components best suited to your organizational needs.

_____

_____

_____

_____

_____

We recommend that you continue to examine the compatibility of the organization's vision, mission, and goals with the framework you have selected. The next segment will provide you with teaming tools that can be incorporated into any framework you choose in order to maximize the effectiveness of all the teams within the organization.

TEAMING TOOLS TO INCREASE TEAM FITNESS

The following tools are a collection of fundamental teaming characteristics assembled from well-known teaming resources. These are tools that teams should collect for their toolbox to enhance team effectiveness.

Figure 5.1 Teaming Assessment

Consider the degree to which you and your team contribute to the following characteristics of teaming. Indicate this in a five-point scale, with five being "full implementation" and zero indicating "not at all."

_____ Team vision and philosophy: What do we believe? What are our values?
The team has determined and demonstrated a shared vision, mission, goals, values, and beliefs.

_____ Team governance: How do we make decisions?
Leadership roles of members of the team are defined. (Examples: facilitator, recorder, timekeeper, liaison, etc.). Planning time for the team is used effectively and is guided by agreed-upon ground rules/principles.

_____ Procedures: How do we function as a team?
All members participate in team meetings toward a clearly identified agenda, tasks, and goals. A team agenda is designed to identify tasks and topics for discussion. Team meeting minutes are recorded and distributed to other appropriate members of the community.

_____ Team identity: Who are we? What do we stand for? How do we recognize our successes?
A team name, logo, motto, and operating principles all contribute to the identity of the team and the accomplishment of its goals.

_____ Communication: How do we keep team members and others informed?
A wide variety of communication is used to effectively interact and exchange ideas with and among all members of the team and the learning community. All members are encouraged to share ideas, and varied views are welcome and respected.

_____ Curriculum: What and how do we learn?
Clear learning goals are established, measured, and revisited often with all team members.

_____ Accountability: How do we measure and assess what is being accomplished?
Team progress is assessed through team effectiveness tools and discussions. Goals are reviewed and measured in order to foster learning and growth.

_____ Teacher efficacy: What are the personal benefits of teaming for me?
Each team member is able to identify ways he/she can be successful both individually and within the school community because of teaming. Individual members and the team are successful, collaborative, and make a positive impact on the school community.

_____ Total

Reflections:

_____

_____

_____

_____

_____

Table 5.2   Creating a Professional Learning Community: Teaming Frameworks and Tools (Examples)

Teaming Tools	Shared Vision, Mission, and Values	Collective Inquiry	Collaborative Teams	Action Orientation and Experimentation	Continuous Improvement	Results Orientation
Team purpose, mission, and beliefs	The team has a written mission and beliefs					
Goal setting					Individual and team goals established	
Team operating principles			Operating principles defined			
Team roles and responsibilities				The role of technology specialist is assigned to collect data on effectiveness of new math curriculum		
Meeting effectiveness						Minutes are reviewed as evidence of the effectiveness of the agenda
Communication			Team minutes are distributed to other teams in the organization			
Team products		All team members will complete teaming inventory				

Team Purpose/Identity

A team's purpose is that which it was created to do. The identity of a group evolves as members work to achieve their purpose. Team-building activities represent a deliberate effort to build a team's identity. Collaboration and trust are the products of continuous team-building efforts. Team building can be challenging, because it requires skills in group dynamics as well as individual relationships.

Successful team building and effective group dynamics foster the development of the team's purpose: "The best teams invest a tremendous amount of time and effort exploring, shaping, and agreeing on a purpose that belongs to them both collectively and individually" (Katzenbach & Smith 1993, 50). Figure 5.2 depicts an example from a team in a graduate leadership class. This example will assist teams in establishing their identity through a team name, symbol, beliefs, roles, and guiding principles. This team activity addresses questions such as: Who are we? What do we believe? What are our roles? What are our guiding principles? The tools that we provide in this section will address all of these questions. Once teams have established these basic elements of team identity, the next

Figure 5.2   Defining and Establishing Team Purpose and Identity: Educational Leadership Class, Team Four-Square Identity

TEAM NAME AND MOTTO	ROLES
The Mixers "Come for the pie, stay for the education" 	We are all the Bakers ~Recorder: ~Liaison: ~Technology Rep: ~Materials: ~Facilitator:
TEAM BELIEFS ~ Children are our future ~ Every ingredient is vital for success ~ Leadership guides the process ~ We believe that mixing together everyone's ideas creates a great team ~ We believe that ideas will be sprinkled in a safe environment	**MIXER GUIDING PRINCIPLES** "Our recipe for success" ~ Wash your hands and begin with open minds ~ Add equal parts of contribution and responsibility to team ~ Mix in mutual support and respect ~ Spice it up with a pinch of risk taking ~ Mix all with joint decision making

step is to establish a team vision and mission. A shared vision provides a clear picture of the ideal destination that all team members agree upon. Consider reviewing vision and mission development in chapter 3. Teams can implement the same strategies to create a shared team vision and mission. Think of teams within your organization. Identify one team and describe its purpose:

_____

_____

_____

Guiding Principles for Teams

Guiding principles are self-imposed agreements that teams create to maintain focus and attention on their purposes. Without these guidelines groups may lose sight of them. These principles allow groups to self-govern in order to minimize individual or group dysfunctional behavior. Basically, guiding principles are established to clarify what will or will not occur within the group. How will group members conduct themselves during team meetings? What do teams expect from each team member? Once guiding principles have been established, the team should continually assess and modify these principles as needed. Figure 5.3 depicts an example of a district leadership team's guiding principles. Describe some formal or informal guiding principles that you have used during your teaming experiences.

_____

_____

_____

_____

Team Performance Goals and Action Strategies

Team goals and action strategies must be established in order to accomplish the group's purpose: "The directional intensity so necessary for successful team performance comes from continuing integration of purpose and performance goals" (Katzenbach & Smith 1993, 56). A team's purpose will determine the types of goals that need to be created and the time required to attain the goals. Team goals must be mutually agreed upon and articulated so that all members are committed to the same outcomes. A guiding question to consider when establishing team goals is, What do we need to do to achieve our purpose? The SMART goal strategy was shared with you in chapter 3; this method states that goals should be specific, measurable, attainable, results oriented, and time bound. Team goals should be both realistic and idealistic. Goals should be stated to allow for teams to stretch for the ideal while also supporting the organizational purpose. They should be written in a way to allow for celebrating small successes as well as total goal attainment. Figure 5.4 depicts a sample of district administrative team goals utilizing the SMART goal strategy.

Choose a team that you are participating on and identify one team goal. Restate the goal using the SMART strategy for goal setting:

I will improve _____ (specific, measurable item) by _____ (how much—an attainable amount) by _____ (when).

Action strategies need to be established to allow for goal attainment. Many schools are mandated

Figure 5.3   District Leadership Team Guiding Principles

We will . . .
- always start and end on time.
- honor one another by being present and participative.
- respect others' opinions.
- assume positive intentions from members of the team.
- take responsibility for our own learning.
- challenge ideas, not people.
- strive for on-task discussions with limited side conversations.
- always honor confidential conversations and idea sharing.
- keep our focus on student and organizational success.
- have fun.

Figure 5.4   Leadership Goals for District Leadership Team, 2004–2005

GOAL 1

We will *identify strengths and skills of each team member* by conducting a written self-assessment of leadership competencies by October 15.

GOAL 2

Each principal will *collect five cultural artifacts that represent best practices in Standard 2 to share with the rest of the team* by November 12.

GOAL 3

Each team member will *complete a mentoring agreement with a colleague to assist in building a successful mentoring relationship* by November 1.

---

by state and federal law to create and implement a school improvement plan. This plan consists of three to four goals, which include action strategies to achieve each organizational goal. We would like to suggest that teams develop their own team improvement plan, to consist of team goals, action strategies, time lines, needed resources, and responsibilities of team members. A team improvement plan is a visual measurement tool that holds the team accountable for reaching their goals. See table 5.3 as an example of a second-grade team goal from a team improvement plan.

Team Roles and Responsibilities

Teams can maximize productivity when using a "divide-and-conquer" approach. Members often determine roles and responsibilities by analyzing individual strengths. Common roles among many

Table 5.3   Team Improvement Plan

Team Goals	Action Strategies	Timeline	Resources	Goal Manager
Goal 1 We will raise our writing scores by 5% on the district writing assessment	Teachers will identify specific writing skills for their students by utilizing the four-square writing technique	Conduct writing activities daily and provide data to team and principal	School improvement planning days will be designated for team members	Second grade team leader
Goal 2				
Goal 3				
Goal 4				

teams include a facilitator, recorder, reporter, timekeeper, and liaison. Team purpose and identity may necessitate alternative roles. For example, some teams may establish an identity of celebrating success and create a role of celebration director. Another example may be an ad hoc committee, which would have different roles and responsibilities than a district leadership team. Some team responsibilities require collaboration with other teams and individuals within the organization.

Meeting Management

Team meetings are an opportunity for teams to communicate, build relationships, and work effectively toward their purposes. An effective meeting utilizes guiding principles, roles and responsibilities, agendas, and meeting minutes. Fundamental to every meeting is an agenda, which should be circulated prior to the meeting. This agenda should include topics for discussion, who will present each topic, and time allotted for each. The quality of the agenda determines the quality of the meeting. Meeting minutes, the written outcome of each agenda topic, hold the team accountable for achieving the agenda goals. These minutes serve as a means of communication and evidence of decisions and accomplishments. An effective organization should provide a meeting management template to all teams. The successful meeting merges the seven teaming tools as illustrated in a template provided in figure 5.5.

Communication: Internal and External

Communication is a key component of teaming success. Teams must be able to communicate both internally and externally with each other, other teams, stakeholders, and the administration. Internal communication is more likely to be successful when teams utilize guiding principles, roles and responsibilities, and effective meeting management. Strong communication skills strengthen relationships.

Communication methods that teams may use internally and externally include: one-on-one discussions, small groups, large groups, e-mail, phone conversations, team minutes, and memos. One effective external communication tool may be team minute distribution. When each team shares their minutes with other teams, it keeps colleagues informed about what is happening within the organization.

Accountability

"Team accountability is about the sincere promises we make to ourselves and others, promises that underpin two critical aspects of teams: commitment and trust. . . . By following through on such a promise, we preserve and extend the trust upon which any team must be built" (Katzenbach & Smith 1993, 60). Consider the following three questions as potential assessments for how well the team contributes to the organization: How does your team measure goal attainment? How do you assess the effectiveness of teaming process? In what ways do you evaluate team performance?

One of the least developed areas in teaming is a measurement or assessment of team performance, processes, and products. This can be quickly explained by the lack of consistent or systematic teaming tools that are used by schools or organizations. Once a teaming model is systematically implemented, it becomes natural, and even likely, that an assessment method will follow. For example, if Arnold and Stevenson's model is implemented, it would be likely that an assessment be created that measures the eight teaming characteristics. An example of this assessment is found in figure 5.1.

The concept of *what gets measured gets done* would suggest the importance of using some form of teaming assessment. When teams are committed to a common purpose, assessment and account-

Figure 5.5   Team Meeting Template

Team Name _____

Date _____

Team Purpose _____

Team Guidelines

_____

_____

_____

Roles and Responsibilities

_____

_____

_____

_____

Agenda (Format will depend on the individual team's purpose.)

_____

_____

_____

_____

_____

Basic required items:

- Topics for discussion
- Presenter for each topic
- Time allotment for each topic

Good agendas may also include:

- Background information
- Items to prepare in advance
- Meeting objectives

Meeting minutes: Agendas may be designed to allow space for the recorder to write.
Basic requirements:

- Every meeting needs to be recorded and disseminated to appropriate personnel
- Minutes should be concise and conclusive

Good minutes may also include:

- A notation, which delineates between discussion, information, or action items.
- Upcoming agenda ideas

ability are welcome. Accountability can be rewarding when teams are intrinsically motivated. Teaming assessments are provided in figures 5.6 and 5.7.

RELATIONSHIP MANAGEMENT

Personal relationships are a shared responsibility for each individual, team, and the leaders of an organization. However, the term *relationship management* has been used to describe the responsibility of the collaborative leader: "It is the purposeful exercise of behavior, communication, and organizational resources to affect the perspective, beliefs, and behaviors of another to influence that person's relationship with you and your collaborative enterprise" (Rubin 2002, 18). Transformational leaders are aware of the need to build individual relationships, positive teams structures, and organizational systems that enhance human relations. Relationship management does not occur by accident or incidentally. Professional development should be provided to teams to share strategies for strengthening and managing teaming relationships. Teams that are proactive about establishing relationships and learning about their colleagues maximize their contributions and minimize the likelihood of team conflicts.

LEADERSHIP IN ACTION

This chapter features nine examples of teaming tools for leaders to put into action:

- Figure 5.1—Teaming Assessment
- Table 5.2—Creating a Professional Learning Community
- Figure 5.2—Defining and Establishing Team Purpose and Identity
- Figure 5.3—District Leadership Team Guiding Principles
- Figure 5.4—Leadership Goals for District Leadership Team
- Figure 5.3—Team Improvement Plan
- Figure 5.5—Team Meeting Template
- Figure 5.6—Team Self-Evaluation
- Figure 5.7—Teaming Assessment

Figure 5.6   Team Self-Evaluation

School Year _____

Team Name _____ Grade Level _____

Directions: As a team please discuss and rate each statement as to where you are as a team for each quarter. Please use the following scale:

N: Concept is not evident.
D: We have dabbled with the concept, but the concept is not a regular practice.
P: The concept is a regular practice.
M: Our team has mastered this concept.

Team Expectation

	School Year_____ Quarter				School Year_____ Quarter				School Year_____ Quarter			
	1	2	3	4	1	2	3	4	1	2	3	4
Our team developed goals, a vision statement, and a handbook.												
Our team coordinated major project due dates.												
Our team conducts meetings that are structured, purposeful, and productive.												
Our team has built relationships with one another.												
Our team communicates with the entire school community.												
Our team has identified roles of the team members.												
Our team shares information regarding needs of students.												
Our team plans activities for professional growth.												
Our team creates agendas and records minutes for all team meetings.												

Figure 5.7   Teaming Assessment

Team Name _____ or circle your team below

> Building Leadership Team   District Leadership Team   District Cabinet
> Curricular Committee   Grade Level Team   Parent Organization
> Other District Level Committee   Other Building Level Committee
> Department Team   District Task Force   Other _____

RATING SCALE

Using a zero-to-five scale, with zero being "nonexistent" and five being "fully implemented," please rate your teaming characteristics.

Teaming Assessment

Teaming Components	1	2	3	4	5
Team purpose: vision, mission, and beliefs					
Team goals					
Roles and responsibilities					
Guiding principles governance					
Communication					
Relationship building and maintenance					
Team achievements and assessments					

Team Fitness Score: _____
Team Fitness Scale:

- 31–35 = 90% World Series champions
- 28–30 = 80% division champions
- 24–27 = 70% minor leaguers
- 21–23 = 60% sandlot team
- 20–0 = 50% sleeping in late but dreaming of playing ball someday.

TEAM GOALS

Using the zero-to-five scale above, establish a score for each of your goals at the end of each quarter.

Team Goals

Team Goals	First Quarter	Second Quarter	Third Quarter	Fourth Quarter
Goal 1				
Goal 2				
Goal 3				

OBSTACLES AND KEYS

Relationship management can be an obstacle if individuals are not trained to communicate and resolve conflicts effectively. Conflicts can arise even when individuals work together toward a common purpose, because of their diverse beliefs and values. It is imperative to a team's success to create and sustain guiding principles to support cohesive and professional relationships. Many resources are available to assist teams to strengthen relationships.

The key for successful teaming is for an organization to adopt a consistent framework and tools to be utilized by all teams. When teams function on-purpose and utilize a common teaming approach, the organization runs like a fine, well-oiled machine. When the organization and each team and aligns visions, beliefs, and goals, the result will be higher levels of performance and success for all. Leaders must make teaming a priority; in return, teams are going to have to make the organization a priority. John Maxwell (2001a, 255) describes the benefits of teaming as

My team makes me better than I am.
My team multiples my value to others.
My team enables me to do what I do best.
My team gives me more time.
My team represents me where I cannot go.
My team provides community for our enjoyment.
My team fulfills the desire of my heart.

LEADERSHIP EXERCISES

The following exercises will assist you in the growth and development of your leadership skills. You will be asked to identify evidence or artifacts that showcase your leadership performance. You are encouraged to utilize these exercises both individually and collectively within your school community.

Exercise 5.1   Four-Square Activity

The Four-Square Activity is a visual process to identify outcomes of four teaming activities. A team should complete this activity together to determine its teaming beliefs, team name and symbol, team vision shield (see chapter 3), and a list of teaming artifacts that show evidence of best practices. This activity works best if the team uses big chart paper and markers to create a large visual for all to see.

TEAM BELIEF

_____
_____
_____
_____
_____
_____

STEAM NAME AND
SYMBOL

_____
_____
_____
_____
_____
_____

TEAM VISION SHIELD

_____
_____
_____
_____
_____

TEAMING EVIDENCE

_____
_____
_____
_____
_____

Exercise 5.2   Artifact

Identify artifacts or evidence of teaming processes within your organization. Locate or create an artifact to place in your leadership journey album. One artifact may be an agenda from a team or committee meeting. Other artifacts schools leaders have identified that illustrate their team-building capabilities are teaming assessments, team minutes, and committee newsletters. Take a minute to jot down a few of your teaming artifacts that will be placed in your journey album.

_____

_____

_____

Exercise 5.3   Reflective Practice

How will you utilize the teaming tools from this chapter to strengthen your teaming and committee work within your organization? How might you share these teaming strategies with stakeholders in your school?

_____

_____

_____

_____

_____

_____

_____

Dear Diary,

Throughout my lifetime I have been keenly aware of the value and benefits of teaming. This was first impressed on me being raised in a family of seven on a dairy farm where every day required team-work. Secondly, my experiences in college athletics reinforced the importance of teaming. Today, as I coach school leaders, I find myself constantly being reminded of teaming for success.

Phil Jackson is one of my favorite coaching mentors and an expert on teaming. In addition to his numerous championship titles he has written an inspiring book of his experiences and philosophies called Sacred Hoops *(Jackson & Deleharty, 1995). Even non–sports enthusiasts would surely be moved by insights of the human spirit conveyed in this best seller.*

The following is a passage from Sacred Hoops *that quotes Rudyard Kipling on the importance of teaming:*

> *Now this is the Law of the Jungle—*
> *As old and as true as the sky;*
> *And the Wolf that shall keep it may prosper,*
> *But the Wolf that shall break it must die.*
> *As the creeper that girdles the tree trunk,*
> *The Law runneth forward and back—*
> *For the strength of the pack is the Wolf,*
> *And the strength of the Wolf is the Pack.*

Kris

RESOURCES

Arnold, J., & C. Stevenson (1998). *Teachers' Teaming Handbook: A Middle Level Planning Guide.* Orlando, Fla.: Harcourt Brace.

Bolman, L., & R. Deal (2003). *Reframing Organizations: Artistry, Choice, and Leadership.* San Francisco: Jossey-Bass.

DuFour, R., & R. Eaker (1998). *Professional Learning Communities at Work: Best Practices for Enhancing Student Achievement.* Bloomington, Ind.: National Education Service.

Jackson, P., & H. Delehanty (1995). *Sacred Hoops: Spiritual Lessons of a Hardwood Warrior.* New York: Hyperion.

Katzenbach, J., & D. Smith (1993). *The Wisdom of Teams: Creating the High Performance Organization.* New York: HarperCollins.

Leithwood, K., D. Jantzi, & R. Steinbach (1999). *Changing Leadership for Changing Times.* Philadelphia: Open University Press.

Maxwell, J. (2001b). *The 17 Indisputable Laws of Teamwork.* Nashville, Tenn.: Thomas Nelson.

Rubin, H. (2002). *Collaborative Leadership: Developing Effective Partnerships in Communities and Schools.* Thousand Oaks, Calif.: Corwin.

Scholtes, P. (1988). *The Team Handbook.* Madison, Wis.: Joiner.

6

SCHOOL CULTURE: CHARTING YOUR LEADERSHIP

It has been said that a fish would be the last creature on earth to discover water, so totally and continuously immersed in it is he. The same might be said of school people working within their culture.

—Barth 2001, 10

LEADERSHIP QUALITIES: SERVANTHOOD, RELATIONSHIPS, AND TEAMWORK

Guiding Questions

What is cultural leadership?
How can you assess your cultural fitness?
In what ways can the school leader change or influence the school culture?

Transformational Leadership Fitness Areas

1 Provides a shared vision and goals
3 Fosters commitment
4 Provides individualized support

SIGHTS TO SEE

The norms, values, and beliefs of the people who make up the organization are often subtle, but they add up to what we know as *culture*. If you walk into a positive and high-functioning organizational culture you know it immediately. There is a spirit of collaboration and synergy that is quickly recognized but not easily explained. It is broadly accepted that the culture of an organization is essential to its success; however, many leaders do not have the tools to develop and sustain an effective culture. It is not difficult to identify a challenging or toxic culture. The complex issues that leaders face are how to define, diagnose, and prescribe cultural components to create a healthy culture. Much as in a family, the features found in each organizational culture are unique, and leaders must work with this "family" to create a nurturing environment. This chapter will guide leaders to collectively identify a cultural definition, descriptors, and strategies to attain a high-performing culture. Much as when we travel in a foreign country, it is important to know the language, conditions, and customs of the people who live there.

This chapter will examine the importance for school leaders of knowing the culture in order to eventually influence, change, or sustain it. We will provide you with a variety of formal and informal definitions, indicators of healthy and toxic cultures, and tools to strengthen your organizational culture. A variety of frameworks will once again be offered that will help you learn and teach others about culture. Southwest Airlines, the leadership standards, and professional learning communities provide examples of healthy cultural norms, values, and practices. "Leadership in Action" will feature a district-level leadership team that redefined cultural leadership.

WHY CULTURAL LEADERSHIP?

Culture reflects the values and beliefs that are demonstrated by members of a community or organization. Cultural leadership is the opportunity to guide, develop, and sustain the culture of an organization. This may be envisioned as a path to achieving the organizational purpose. If the leader and members of this organization are not on the same path, there is little chance the organization will achieve its ultimate purpose. The first step for a leader is to uncover or take inventory of the norms embedded in the history of the organization.

Every culture has stated and unstated norms that govern how its members will perform. Awareness of the organizational norms and values provides a gauge for how a culture can be modified or sustained. Often new leaders enter organizations with preconceived goals that may not be compatible with the existing cultures. The transformational leader possesses a cultural compass to facilitate relationship building in a way that contributes to a shared vision and a healthy organizational culture. A transformational leader does not attempt to change culture but rather works to study and understand its members and their collective values. If a school seeks learning as its greatest value, it must define learning as among its most important norms and beliefs.

Leaders leading leaders is a desired characteristic of most organizations, but it is a difficult one to achieve. Michael Fullan (2004) highlights the importance of developing cultural leadership: "Good leaders foster good leadership at other levels. Leaders at other levels produce a steady stream of future leaders for the whole system" (8). Those who desire shared leadership must first consider whether their own leadership is compatible with the existing beliefs of individuals, teams, and the organization. Since collaborative leadership is an indicator of a healthy culture, a leader may begin to establish practices that invite and empower members to assume shared leadership roles.

The first five *essentials* in this leadership journey are a leadership fitness program, action-based belief development, a shared vision and mission, leadership standards, and team-building frameworks. Each essential encourages you to consider three levels of leadership: individual, team, and organizational.

Individual Fitness >>>>>>	Team Fitness >>>>>>	Organizational Fitness
Beliefs >>>>>>	Beliefs >>>>>>	Beliefs
Vision >>>>>>	Vision >>>>>>	Vision

We hope that you will deepen your understanding of culture as you relate it to these levels of leadership. We encourage you to first identify the features of your culture and then determine strategies to increase your individual, team, and organizational cultural fitness.

DEFINING CULTURE: FORMAL AND INFORMAL DESCRIPTIONS

Many definitions attempt to explain culture. Generally, culture is defined as the shared norms, beliefs, values, and customs of the members of the organization. The following are formal descriptions that illustrate the diversity of language and perspective that are used to define culture:

_____ "Culture is often described as the way things get done around here" (Deal & Kennedy 1982, 4).

_____ "The culture becomes what it is over time as people cope with problems, establish routines and rituals, and develop traditions and ceremonies that strengthen and sustain the underlying norms, values, and beliefs" (Deal & Peterson, 1999, 51).

_____ "In school cultures valuing collegiality and collaboration, there is a better climate for the social and professional exchange of ideas, the enhancement and spread of effective practices, and widespread professional problem solving" (Deal & Peterson 1999, 7).

_____ Culture is the inner reality that "reflects what organizational members care about, what they are willing to spend time doing, what and how they celebrate, and what they talk about" (Robbins and Alvy 1995, 23).

_____ Culture is a school's "unwritten rules and traditions, norms, and expectations that seem to permeate everything: the way people act, how they dress, what they talk a bout or avoid talking about, whether they seek out colleagues for help or don't, and how teachers, feel about their work and their students" (Deal & Peterson 1999, 2).

Informal descriptions of culture provide leaders with a user-friendly approach to this complex organizational feature. While it may be challenging to understand and define your own culture, the following descriptions by leaders may sound familiar:

_____ Staff explores and embraces change ideas.

_____ We celebrate together.

_____ The staff lounge is used as a place to complain about what's wrong around here.

_____ Student discipline is at the center of almost every discussion within the building.

_____ The principal is rarely seen in the hallways or the classrooms.

_____ Staff finds out about changes after they have already been decided; we either jump on board or we are left behind.

_____ The walls in our schools tell our story about our learning community.

_____ Parents play an integral part in our school day; they volunteer and tutor and are often dropping in to provide support.

_____ Students are encouraged to find their passion for learning and create learning opportunities for themselves.

_____ Things always seem like top-down leadership. The higher ups tell us what we are supposed to do and we do it.

_____ We all work so collaboratively on every project that we are presented with. You can't walk through this building without seeing colleagues working alongside one another to ensure student success.

More important than determining a single meaning of culture is to create or build a shared cultural definition. Consider which of these formal definitions or informal descriptions most accurately define your organizational culture. Place a check mark alongside the definitions or statements that best describe your culture. Within each definition you have checked, circle the words or phrases that are most distinct to your organization. Would other members of your team, department, or organization select the same ones? Write your own organizational definition of culture using these words and phrases in the space below:

_____

_____

_____

Once you have determined your individual definition of culture, we encourage you to complete the activity again with a group of colleagues. Collectively identify the key words, phrases, and definitions that best describe your culture.

_____

_____

_____

What were the similar components of the definitions?

_____

_____

What were differences among your cultural definitions?

_____

_____

FRAMEWORKS THAT SHAPE AND DEFINE CULTURE

Frameworks can be used in order to shape and understand culture. A menu of frameworks has been used throughout this leadership guide to provide organizational alternatives. Table 6.1 illustrates five frameworks that support culture building as a visual and tangible starting point for organizations.

PROFESSIONAL LEARNING COMMUNITIES

The six comprehensive features of this model can substantiate the selection of Dufour and Eaker's "professional learning communities" as a framework for cultural leadership. As you explore this framework in *Professional Learning Communities at Work: Best Practices for Enhancing Student Achievement* (1998), you will find a wealth of cultural strategies for school reform, the change pro-

Table 6.1 Frameworks That Shape and Define Culture

Deal and Peterson: Cultural Benefits	DuFour and Eaker: Professional Learning Communities	ISLLC Leadership Standard 2: School Culture	Southwest Airlines: Cultural Norms	Leithwood Transformational Leadership
Effectiveness and productivity	Shared vision, mission mission, and values	Learning is aligned with vision and mission	Be visionary	Create a shared vision
Collegiality and collaboration	Collective Inquiry	Life long learning is valued and modeled	Celebrate everything	Model best practices
Change and improvement	Collaborative teams	Achievements are recognized and celebrated	Hire the right people	Foster commitment
Energy and motivation	Action, orientation, and experimentation	High expectations established and maintained	Dare to be different	Provide individual support
Commitment and identity	Continuous improvement	Professional growth is valued and assessed	Keep a warrior spirit	Enhance professional growth
Priorities defined	Results orientation	Culture and climate continually assessed		Establish and maintain high expectations

cess, and continuous improvement. Since language can also be characteristic of a culture, notice the unique language of this model: *collective inquiry, action research, professional collaboration, collaborative teams,* and *results orientation.* Educators have equated the description of professional learning communities to an ideal cultural definition: "The most promising strategy for sustained, substantive school improvement is developing the ability of school personnel to function as professional learning communities" (DuFour & Eaker 1998, xi). It is not surprising that this model is supported by such organizations as the Hope Foundation and the National Educational Service.

CULTURAL BENEFITS

Prominent cultural authors Terrance Deal and Kent Peterson's *Shaping School Culture* (1999, 7–8) provides a synopsis of the many functions and benefits of school culture. The main features of this cultural framework are listed below in detail.

_____ *Culture fosters school effectiveness and productivity.* Organizational members are productive when a culture focuses on productivity, performance, and improvement.

_____ *Culture improves collegial and collaborative activities that foster better communication and problem solving.* This culture emphasizes collegiality, socialization, and collaboration to improve problem solving and performance.

_____ *Culture fosters successful change and improvement efforts.* Risk taking, experimentation, and innovation are characterized in a culture of change.

_____ *Culture builds commitment and identity.* Commitment and motivation increase in an environment where the mission is clear and inspiring. Cultures with shared values, socialization, and caring enhance the identity of an organization.

_____ *Culture increases the energy, motivation, and vitality of a school staff, students, and community.* A social environment promotes workers who are optimistic and energetic.

_____ *Culture increases the focus of daily behavior and attention on what is important and valued.* Informal and unwritten values are illustrated through the actions of the organizational members.

As a means to assess your understanding of your cultural fitness, rate each item above on a scale of zero to five. Identify your strong areas as a five, mediocre areas as four or three, and areas of improvement with a rating of two or one. Select an area of strength and identify examples that can be found within your school culture.

_____

_____

_____

_____

ISLLC STANDARD 2

Leadership standards provide leaders with another framework to understand and assess culture. Standard 2 was introduced in chapter 4 and is featured as a cultural framework. The second leadership standard addresses the significance of school culture: *The competent school administrator is an educational leader who promotes the success of all students by advocating, nurturing, and sustaining a school culture and instructional program conducive to student learning and staff professional growth.* This standard includes forty indicators with a focus on cultural collaboration and professional learning opportunities. A partial list of indicators considered as best practices found in Standard 2 are listed below:

_____ All individuals are treated with fairness, dignity, and respect.

_____ Professional development promotes a focus on student learning consistent with the school vision and goals.

_____ Students and staff feel valued and important.

_____ The responsibilities and contributions of each individual are acknowledged.

_____ Barriers to student learning are identified, clarified, and addressed.

_____ Lifelong learning is encouraged and modeled.

_____ There is a culture of high expectations for self, student, and staff performance.

_____ Student and staff accomplishments are recognized and celebrated.

_____ Diversity is considered in developing learning experiences.

_____ Technologies are used in teaching and learning.

_____ Multiple opportunities to learn are available to all students.

_____ The school is organized and aligned for success.

_____ Curricular, cocurricular, and extracurricular programs are designed, implemented, evaluated, and refined.

_____ Curriculum decisions are based on research, expertise of teachers, and the recommendations of learned societies.

_____ The school culture and climate are assessed on a regular basis.

_____ A variety of sources of information is used to make decisions.

_____ Student learning is assessed using a variety of techniques.

_____ Multiple sources of information regarding performance are used by staff and students.
_____ A variety of supervisory and evaluation models are employed.
_____ Pupil programs are developed to meet the needs of students and their families.

In chapter 4 you completed the standards assessment. Review the indicators above from an organizational perspective. Place a plus sign next to each indicator that exists within your organizational culture. Place a minus sign next to each indicator that you do not see in existence in your culture. Did you have more plus or minus cultural indicators? Which indicators do you feel need to be strengthened within your culture?

_____

_____

_____

_____

SOUTHWEST AIRLINES MODEL

The Southwest Airlines model can also be utilized to build and maintain a healthy culture. Southwest has been cited as an American success story and has been featured in numerous books and periodicals, such as _Forbes, Business Week,_ and the _Wall Street Journal._ Authors Kevin and Jackie Freiberg capture the culture and essence of Southwest Airline's success in _Nuts! Southwest Airlines' Crazy Recipe for Business and Personal Success_ (1996). Innovative and courageous leadership early in the company's history produced a well-defined purpose and core values. Southwest describes its values as the "emotional rules that govern our behavior and attitudes. Values determine our choices, including those we make in an organizational context. . . . If we wanted to learn more about your values, we would ask to see two things: your checkbook and your calendar. How you spend your money and time tells us a lot about what you value" (Freiberg & Freiberg 1996, 146).

The Southwest philosophy is described as the "quality and character of interactions with colleagues and the degree of fun, creativity, and enthusiasm" employees bring to the job (Freiberg & Freiberg 1996, 151). The statements shown in the cultural framework describe the unique spirit and collaboration that is held in high esteem for Southwest Airlines: _Be visionary. Celebrate everything. Hire the right people. Keep a warrior spirit._ This cultural framework is designed for healthy cultures that want to further develop their organizational wellness.

CULTURAL CHECKUP

The transformational leadership model is also included in the cultural frameworks. These five models have been provided to give you a better understanding of culture and your impact as a leader. While each framework in its entirety represents a cultural theme, commonalities exist across the five models. Review table 6.1: What concepts do you see repeated in the frameworks?

_____

_____

What cultural phraseology is repeated in the various frameworks?

_____

_____

What concepts do you find most suitable to your culture?

_____

_____

What other models or frameworks might you use to examine your culture?

_____

_____

What are the next steps you will take to develop, change, or sustain your culture?

_____

_____

Whom will you involve in the initial cultural conversations?

_____

_____

CULTURAL FITNESS LEVEL: HEALTHY OR TOXIC?

In this chapter we have provided you with information and insights that may enable you to identify and define healthy cultural features. If you already work within a healthy culture, you know it and will want to sustain and build upon its strengths. If you are in a toxic culture, you too are keenly aware of your conditions but may be unclear as to how to modify or transform the negativity that permeates the organization. A toxic culture may have such underlying behaviors as jealousy, criticism, and resistance to change. Once again Deal and Peterson (1999) provide practical strategies that may be helpful to leaders who encounter degrees or components of a negative culture. Deal and Peterson suggest "antidotes for negativism" (1999, 127), shown below:

- Confront the negativity; give people a chance to openly express their sentiments; shield and support positive staff and elements.
- Focus energy on the recruitment, selection, and retention of effective, positive staff, continuously celebrate the positive and the possible.
- Consciously and directly attempt to eliminate the negative and replace it with positive norms.
- Develop new norms of success and renewal.
- Attempt to identify and relocate personnel to a different environment where they may be more successful and compatible with the culture.

Overcoming and transforming a negative culture requires well planned action. Understanding the reasons for resistance and utilizing Deal and Peterson's six antidotes are the first actions a leader should take. Much of the literature on culture proposes that to change culture requires relationship management. "Changing systems means changing people . . . and that influencing change in other people only occurs by managing our relationships with them" (Rubin 2002, 38). A leader has the opportunity and responsibility to influence the culture and begins by understanding the existing culture and finding ways to either maximize the positive or modify toxic components. The transformational leader will not attempt to transform culture without transforming the relationships that constitute it.

CULTURAL CHANGE: GROWTH OR RESISTANCE?

Everyone within an organization must attend to structural and cultural change. Dufour and Eaker (1998) offer an explanation of structure and culture in order to differentiate change efforts: "The structure of an organization is founded upon its politics, procedures, rules, and relationships. The culture of an organization is founded upon the assumptions, beliefs, values, and habits that constitute the norms for that organization" (131). It is not surprising, therefore, that changing long-standing beliefs, values, and habits is challenging. Change also requires letting go of the status quo and adopting something new in its place. This frequently causes emotional responses of resistance, fear, and frustration. The topic of change could fill an entire chapter. For our purposes, we will suggest that effective leaders shape rather than change culture, teach others about the process and stages of cultural change, build support for shared values, and cultivate an environment of learning.

LEADERSHIP IN ACTION

This section describes an administrative leadership team that utilized the six areas of transformational leadership to increase individual, team, and cultural leadership capacity. The superintendent, who had exercised his own transformational leadership fitness, realized the importance of strengthening the leadership team around him. Traditional sit-and-get meetings, conducted solely by the superintendent, were redesigned to develop team building through engaged and reflective learning for sixteen district administrators—central office staff, principals, and assistant principals. A major challenge facing this team was a conservative and rural community that had previously rejected two school referendums. These sessions were designed to be interactive and empowering for each leader; their theme was "Leadership: Learning and Leading Together." The goals for each learning session included

- identifying strengths and skills of members of the leadership team and ways the team could maximize mentoring, support, and commitment to each other;
- understanding and utilizing the features of transformational leadership;
- sharing with other members of the leadership team successful teaming strategies at each site or department.

Eight leadership sessions were designed, with input from members of the leadership team and the superintendent. The sessions included professional development planning, defining leadership, team development, conducting effective meetings, mentoring, transformational leadership, building partnerships, and a leadership retreat.

The first leadership session introduced the professional development objectives, with an emphasis on developing individual and team identity. Each participant completed a leadership self-profile during the introduction. This profile assisted leaders to become more aware of their own leadership practices. Collectively, the profiles helped to shape the identity and potential strengths and weaknesses of the leadership team.

One of the first ideas generated by the leadership team was the importance of identifying and celebrating leadership successes. The motto "You Go the Distance for Children" was adopted, along with tennis-shoe pins, to illustrate the commitment of members of the team. At the beginning of each session a colleague, previously awarded the pin, would share another team member's success story and present the pin to him or her.

During a subsequent session the team was introduced to the concept of mentoring as a source of learning, support, and collaboration. Each leader agreed to work with a mentor for the remainder of the year. Tasks agreed upon for each mentor included the following: visit the mentors' school, provide feedback on its school improvement plan, and assist in the pending community referendum. The remaining leadership sessions were hosted at each school site by each of the mentors. This arrangement resulted in each mentor fostering a relationship of trust and support. We will provide additional information on mentoring later in your leadership journey, in chapter 8.

The effort to pass a third referendum became a focus for several of the next leadership sessions. It was during these sessions that the transformational leadership model was introduced to the leadership team. The team discussed the features of transformational leadership and identified ways this model could be used as both a means of leadership development and a tool for building community partnerships. Stakeholders who were considered essential in passing the referendum included the teachers' union, parent groups, retired citizens, and business leaders. Each pair of mentors designed a plan for fostering commitment in the school from the stakeholders, utilizing the transformational leadership model.

During the sessions that followed, leaders defined plans for the referendum, worked with their mentors, and shared successes and challenges of their own leadership journeys. The administrative team concluded the year of "Leading and Learning Together" with the first annual "District of Dreams" retreat. The focus of the day was "Going the Distance" for children; the theme was baseball and teaming. The program for the day included vision building, renewed commitment, relationship building, celebrating successes, and enhancing student achievement through school improvement planning. After nine "innings," each team member had celebrated, reflected, and been reenergized to go the distance for children. At the end of this season it was time for each leader to assess his or her own leadership fitness and plan for the cultural areas to be strengthened and improved upon during the upcoming year.

The following year, using transformational leadership as a blueprint for learning, the leadership team modified the administrative team meetings. With a new focus on learning, the superintendent introduced weekly learning sessions as the new protocol for administrative team meetings. The learning sessions were designed to utilize multiple facilitators, maximize shared leadership, and provide opportunities for collegial conversations. Each learning session opened with shared celebrations and concluded with reflections on the learning accomplishments of the session. No longer were these business meetings run by one person; they were learning sessions conducted by all. As transformational leaders, the team members exercised their leadership skills and became empowered for and engaged and invested in their own learning. Cultural leadership was demonstrated, and it will influence the overall culture as each leader defines his or her role.

OBSTACLES AND KEYS

The main obstacle of culture building is that people will grow comfortable in the status quo and tend not to look beyond their present cultures to search for something better for themselves and the organization. While culture exists in every organization, it is difficult to identify and articulate. New people fail to recognize the culture before they change it. Existing members become like chameleons, blending into their surroundings, rather than taking action to change the colors of their environment.

The key to shaping our culture is to identify a shared meaning. The transformational leader shapes culture one individual at a time. It is through shared meaning that an organization can build leadership capacity and enhance learning.

LEADERSHIP EXERCISES

The following exercises will assist you in the growth and development of your leadership skills. You will be asked to identify evidence or artifacts that showcase your leadership performance. You are encouraged to utilize these exercises both individually and collectively within your school community.

Exercise 6.1 Conducting an Archeological Search for Culture

You have been hired to conduct an archeological search of evidence of your school culture and one of the teams within your organization. A list of possible artifacts, or evidence, is listed in the chart that follows. Describe the evidence you find as you dig beyond the surface of your culture.

Conducting an Archeological Search for Culture

Cultural Evidence and Artifacts	Team Findings	Organizational/School/ Community Findings
Physical environment (space priorities, colors, learning structures, decorations, displays, etc.)		
Language/Communication (name, mission statement, vision, newsletters, greetings, banners, meeting management, diversity, networking, stories, etc.)		
Customs/Traditions (beginnings, historical events, past achievements, music, programs, professional development, etc.)		
Favorite symbols (mascot, logos, artwork, trophies, etc.)		
Celebrations (special events, accomplishments, recognition programs, etc.)		

CULTURAL ASSESSMENT

What were the norms discovered through evidence and artifacts of team culture? Organizational culture?

_____
_____
_____
_____
_____

What did you discover about what is valued most among the team? The organization?
What evidence did you uncover that was a surprise? What evidence reinforced the existing norms of the team or organizational culture?

_____
_____
_____
_____
_____

What is a possible new cultural symbol, event, or celebration that you may want to consider to enhance the future organizational culture?

_____
_____
_____
_____
_____

Exercise 6.2   The Language and Culture of Music: Identifying Your School Culture

Music serves as a means to communicate, influence, and define time periods throughout our lives. Consider how the songs and television themes listed below reflect or describe your school culture. Provide examples that describe your team, department, and school culture for as many songs as possible.

Cheers
M.A.S.H.
Welcome Back, Kotter
Room 222
"Eight Days a Week"
"We Are Family"
Happy Days
One Day at a Time
The Facts of Life
Dynasty
"Miracles Happen"
Mission Impossible
"S.O.S."
"Money. Money. Money"
"The Impossible Dream"
"Take a Chance on Me"
"I Will Survive"
"High Hopes"
"Ain't No Stoppin' Us Now"
"If I Could Fly"

Other songs that describe my school culture:

_____

_____

_____

Exercise 6.3 Southwest Airlines: Culture and Community

Consider ways you could use the following cultural values of Southwest Airlines to strengthen the culture within your own organization. Respond to the following questions and consider ways in which each might be used as a means to enhance your school culture.

Cultural Values

leaders leading leaders   boundary spanners
use conflicts to build relationships   leadership enriches the human spirit
stretch to grow   leading from the inside out   listen for more than you hear
a self-renewing community   high-performance relationships

1. In what ways can members of the school community stretch to grow?

_____

_____

2. How would you as a leader model the concept of *leaders leading leaders?*

_____

_____

3. What strategies will you use to build *high-performance relationships?*

_____

_____

4. What actions can you take to create *boundary spanners?*

_____

_____

5. What do you do as a school leader to *listen for more than you hear?*

_____

_____

6. How do you *use conflicts to build relationships* within the school community?

_____

_____

7. What strategies do you use to create a community that is *self-renewing?*

_____

_____

8. If *leadership enriches the human spirit,* how has your spirit grown through your leadership endeavors?

_____

_____

9. How would you apply the phrase *leading from the inside out* in your organization?

_____

_____

Exercise 6.4   Artifact

Identify artifacts or evidence of your organizational culture. Locate or create an artifact to place in your leadership journey album. One artifact may be found using the archeological culture exercise. Other artifacts identified by school leaders that illustrate culture building are cultural assessments, culture building goals and strategies, and school newsletters. Take a minute to jot down a few of your culture artifacts that will be placed in your journey album.

_____
_____
_____
_____
_____

Exercise 6.5   Reflective Practice

State three goals that you will implement in order to strengthen your cultural fitness.

_____
_____
_____

What framework or model will you utilize to build and foster an understanding of culture with your staff?

_____
_____
_____
_____

Dear Travel Diary,

This chapter was a challenge to write. We realized the importance of culture even before we began to write this book and struggled to put into words the impact that cultural change can have on an organization. We wanted to share as much information with the reader as we could possibly fit into this chapter but realized quickly that unless we wanted to write another book just on culture, we would never fit everything in. At one point we needed to toss twenty-nine pages of manuscript, because, as Kris said, to reorganize what we then had would be like trying to rearrange furniture on the Titanic.

Eventually, we were able to provide definitions and meanings through frameworks and other experts in the field. Ironically, after all of this hard work, we determined that each reader will still have to define culture themselves. This may be the single greatest challenge that school leaders face. It is for me.

Kellie

RESOURCES

Barth, R. (2001). *Learning by Heart*. San Francisco: Jossey-Bass.

Communities of Hope. *The Hope Foundation*. Retrieved September 19, 2004, from www.communities ofhope.org.

Deal, T., & A. Kennedy (1982). *Corporate Cultures: The Rites and Rituals of Corporate Life*. Reading, Mass.: Addison-Wesley.

Deal, T., & K. Peterson (1999). *Shaping School Culture: The Heart of Leadership*. San Francisco: Jossey-Bass.

Deal, T., & K. Peterson (2002). *Shaping School Culture Fieldbook*. San Francisco: Jossey-Bass.

DuFour, R., & R. Eaker (1998). *Professional Learning Communities at Work: Best Practices for Enhancing Student Achievement*. Bloomington, Ind.: National Education Service.

Freiberg, K., & J. Freiberg (1996). *Nuts! Southwest Airlines' Crazy Recipe for Business and Personal Success*. New York: Broadway Books.

Fullan, M. (2004). *Leading in a Culture of Change: Personal Action Guide and Workbook*. San Francisco: Jossey-Bass.

Professional Learning Communities. *National Educational Service*. Retrieved September 19, 2005, from www. solution-tree.com.

Robbins, P., & H. Alvy (1995). *The Principal's Companion: Strategies and Hints to Make the Job Easier*. Thousand Oaks, Calif.: Corwin.

Rubin, H. (2002). *Collaborative Leadership: Developing Effective Partnerships in Communities and Schools*. Thousand Oaks, Calif.: Corwin.

LEADERSHIP VISIBILITY:
A FITNESS WALK IN OUR OWN BACKYARD

The walk-through process is the most powerful qualitative assessment instrument that we have used that recognizes individual students by placing them in one-on-one interaction with an adult to reflect expressively the knowledge and skills they have gained.

—Barnes & Miller 2001, 24

LEADERSHIP QUALITIES: CARING, INITIATIVE, AND MODELING

Guiding Questions

How do fitness walks benefit all members of a school community?
How can fitness walks be utilized within the organization?
How can fitness walks be used to assess organizational goals?

Transformational Leadership Fitness Areas

2 Models behavior and best practices
4 Provides individual support
6 Establishes high performance expectations.

SIGHTS TO SEE

The transformational leader builds relationships and commitments by being highly visible and interactive within the school community. Visible presence is more than about being in attendance—it is about making a difference in the environment by being intentional, interactive, and *impactful*. This visibility is a chance for leaders to *walk their talk* and demonstrate personal and organizational values.

Visible presence models for teachers and staff the leader's commitment to being the lead learner. A leader's presence offers gifts or *presents* of time, commitment, and support. Leadership visibility provides formal and informal opportunities to provide individualized support and build relationships. Examples of informal visibility include the leader who greets students and staff upon arrival to school, attends school-sponsored events, drops into classrooms at the beginning and end of the day, and seeks out one-on-one cafeteria and teacher lounge conversations as often as possible. Effective leaders also utilize purposeful and systematic approaches to visibility.

This chapter will feature the use of learning or fitness walks as a means for leaders to increase visible presence. The term *fitness walk* describes an interactive method for leaders and staff to develop and assess organizational success. The purposes of fitness walks may be building relationships, digging for data, or reading the culture. In any case, the leader must determine the type of walk that is desired to support and sustain the organizational vision, beliefs, and goals. Leadership visibility frameworks illustrate the *intentionality* of the organization to learn and grow. Fitness walks showcase the impact that visible presence can have on the individual and the organization. "Leadership in Action" will share examples of visible presence in a variety of school settings.

FITNESS WALKS: A STROLL IN OUR OWN BACKYARD

Professional growth and development is at the heart of every successful learning community. Unfortunately, educators may often miss the opportunity to learn in their own school communities. Some educators have discovered success with *walk-throughs*. A variety of definitions have been used to describe walk-throughs at the organizational level: "A walk-through creates a schoolwide picture made up of many small snapshots. . . . It's a strategy for providing a school, not an individual teacher, with feedback about what it's doing or not doing." (Richardson 2001, 2). Another definition states, "The walk-through focuses the participants on improving the core of educational practice[;] . . . how teachers understand the nature of knowledge, the student's role in learning; and how these ideas about knowledge and learning manifest themselves in teaching and class work" (Barnes & Miller 2001, 22). The transformational leader may conduct a fitness walk in order to model behavior and best practices, provide individual support, or establish high performance expectations. Fitness walks may benefit a principal, assistant principal, team leader, teacher, special education teacher, student teacher, parent, or community member to obtain a well-rounded view of the school community. This chapter will identify ways in which leaders can enhance visibility through fitness walks in their own backyards.

The Purposes of Fitness Walks

The first step of a fitness walk is to establish an individual, team, or organizational purpose. What do we want to learn about our school? Do we want to examine curriculum integration, instructional strategies, or the cultural environment? Successful fitness walks are clear and purposeful. A few examples of purposes follow:

- To provide opportunities for teachers and school leaders to observe and talk with students engaged in learning events in the classroom
- To increase the visible presence of school leaders to interact in the learning environment of the school

- To provide a time efficient way to view the learning culture of classrooms and the school
- To provide a collaborative opportunity for teachers, parents, and community members to interact and communicate with a focus on student learning
- To observe and assess specific features of curriculum and instruction by observing and conversing with students and teachers

How do you demonstrate leadership visibility within your organization?

_____

_____

_____

_____

What would be the purpose of your leadership fitness walks?

_____

_____

_____

The Frameworks of Fitness Walks

The four frameworks in table 7.1 provide a variety of strategies for implementing or strengthening visible presence. As in the previous chapters, we encourage you to consider using one of the frameworks or combining components of each framework to create a model that works best for your organizational purposes.

The Kouzes and Posner framework provides leaders with a simple but purposeful approach to maximize the benefits of interacting through visibility. Leadership visibility requires not only presence but also attention to what occurs during the interactions. Authors Kouzes and Posner have described as one of the essentials of *Encouraging the Heart* (1999) the importance of paying attention. When leaders pay attention, they put others first. They are intent listeners who have a desire to understand and support others. Each interaction has a clear focus, which results in a means to assess and make successful decisions for the organization.

Three additional frameworks have been provided to assist you in developing fitness walks. Carolyn Downey's (Downey, Steffy, English, Fraser, & Poston 2004) framework for walk-throughs suggests a broad view of instructional practices with the intent to provide informal continuous feedback. This framework encourages the teacher and observer to reflect on what was informally observed. On the other hand, Lauren Resnick's (1995) framework is a formal observation of one particular learning session. Her learning-walk model focuses on best practices of instruction and is written feedback that is presented to the teacher. Lastly, the transformational framework is featured to provide individual support, model best practices, and foster relationship building.

Table 7.1 Visible Presence Frameworks

Transformational Leadership Walk the Vision	Carolyn Downey Walk-Throughs	Lauren Resnick Learning Walks	Kouzes and Posner Pay Attention
Fitness walks focus on observing the organizational vision wherever anyone ventures within the school. Read the walls. What are they telling us?	Focus on everyone using self-reflection, self-diagnosis, and continuous professional growth	Focus primarily on ensuring a particular instructional practice is being implemented	Release the positive. An environment of support and caring is modeled.
The leader models lifelong learning by seeking out new learning practices being implemented within the organization.	Very informal observations (nothing is written up or filed)	Formal write up that may be put in an individual's file	Put others first. Each person feels as though they are central to the organization.
The leader provides individualized support through building and maintaing relationships with members of the school community.	Short 2–3-minute visits	10–20-minute visits	Listen with your eyes and your heart. Leaders visibly interact and listen to affirm the value and contributions of each individual.
The leader supports professional development opportunities by searching for needs of the organization through fitness walks.	Focus on instruction in a general way and not looking for particular instructional practices	Focus on specific researched instructional practices	Hang out. This is the the informal time commitment to pay attention to the concerns and accomplishments of others.
The leader monitors and supports high expectations by utilizing the fitness walks to both determine the organizational expectations and assess achievement.	Uses different levels of feedback: direct, indirect, and interactive	Feedback is primarily direct	Be a friend and open up. Support mutual give and take communication and relationship building.
The leader fosters commitment to the organization by problem solving through a collaborative team fitness walk approach.	Focus is on reflective questions about one's practice—not on the lesson observed	Focus is on the lesson observed and how to improve the lesson and best practices	Seek and ye shall find. The observer determines what they will be looking for and searching for particular data.
	More reflective model at a higher cognitive level for the teacher	More inspectional model of accountability for particular instructional practices	

Which framework or components of a framework have you used within your organizational setting?

_____

_____

_____

Which framework or features would you like to utilize to enhance your visible presence?

_____

_____

_____

Fitness Walks to Build and Maintain Relationships

One of the purposes of a fitness walk is to build and maintain relationships. Leaders have to prioritize how they spend their time due to the great demands that they face. Consider the benefits of fitness walks:

- Time spent with others
- Synergy and unity within the organization
- A sense of calmness in the organization
- An energized and empowered staff
- A staff whose members feel better about themselves and the leader
- Support for individual and organizational purposes
- Trust from the members of the organization
- The capability to inspire others

The collaborative leader values every opportunity to build relationships. Time management experts like Steven Covey teach leaders the importance of dealing with *first things first*, through effective use of two tools—the clock and the compass (Covey, Merrill, & Merrill 1994). Covey et al. suggest that "the clock represents our commitments, schedules, goals, etc. . . . The compass, on the other hand, represents what is important to us. This includes our mission, priorities, and values. The leader constantly struggles for congruence in how to use the clock and the compass" (19). Fitness walks enable leaders to accomplish both.

Fitness Walks to Dig for Data

One way in which organizations assess the attainment of high expectations is to use data collected from fitness walks. "After the walk-through each fall, our teachers analyze the data to determine what skills and understandings are secure for children and which areas require increased attention for the remainder of the year. . . . Teachers, working in small teams and individually, use the data to target their instruction" (Barnes & Miller 2001, 24).

The transformational framework features an example of how an individual or team can collect data that showcases organizational success. The leader utilizes fitness walks to establish both organizational expectations and assess achievement. By visiting instructional settings the leader is able to assess student learning. Those conducting the fitness walk may discuss with the students and teachers the lesson objectives and how these objectives are being measured. Fitness walks to dig for data allow the leader or team to visually assess student engagement and understanding of the lesson objective. A fitness-walk postcard in the "Leadership in Action" segment describes an actual data fitness walk. What data might you or a team search for during a fitness walk?

_____

_____

_____

Fitness Walks to Read the Walls

Reading the walls of the school is one of the main ways to gather information about the organizational culture. In order to gain a more diverse perspective we must determine what others see when they enter our schools. When we plan a fitness walk to read the walls, we need to determine whose eyes we are going to be looking through. Will we be looking through the eyes of students, parents, teachers, community members, or administrators? Each of these groups will view our buildings in different ways, but their impressions are all valued.

The physical and cultural environment of the organization tells a story to everyone who enters the front doors. Would students and parents feel that the environment of the school is warm and inviting or cold and unwelcoming? Are the mission and vision of the school observed through the environment? Are the actions of the organizational members supportive of the mission and vision? How does the display of student work or visual representations contribute to the school culture? What do we hear throughout the school environment? These are just a few questions that fitness walks would address. What does the physical and cultural environment of your school say to those that enter?

_____

_____

_____

_____

LEADERSHIP IN ACTION

Postcard: A Transformational Leadership Fitness Walk

Name: Ms. Hammerle
Date: December 5
Purpose for a walk-through:

__X__ TL [transformational leadership] fitness walk	____ Culture walk
____ Beliefs walk	____ Mentoring walk
____ Vision walk	____ Curricular walk
____ Standards walk	____ Maintenance walk
____ Teaming walk	____ Addressing individual concern
____ Classroom management walk	____ New instructional initiative walk

Reflections: *Ms. Hammerle, you did an excellent job modeling instructional practice to the teachers during the faculty meeting on Tuesday. The interactive activity should be easily adapted so that the teachers can use the practice to teach their students. When teachers can actually participate in a model lesson themselves it makes it easier for them to incorporate the technique into their own instruction. Thank you so much for sharing your expertise.*

Postcard: A Beliefs Fitness Walk

Name: Mrs. Stilp
Date: January 10

Purpose for a walk-through:

____ TL fitness walk   ____ Culture walk
_X_ Beliefs walk   ____ Mentoring walk
____ Vision walk   ____ Curricular walk
____ Standards walk   ____ Maintenance walk
____ Teaming walk   ____ Addressing individual concern
____ Classroom management walk   ____ New instructional initiative walk

Reflections: *Karen, I noticed today when I stopped in at the beginning of the day that you have the students state the school beliefs every morning. You even went on to ask your students to expound on those beliefs and how they relate to their actions. I was very impressed by this and would like to know if you could share this learning strategy with the staff at our next staff learning session. You truly put our beliefs into action and you encourage that action from your students every day. Please let me know how you feel about sharing with the staff.*

Postcard: A Vision Fitness Walk

Name: Mrs. Keck
Date: September 19
Purpose for a walk-through:

____ TL fitness walk   ____ Culture walk
____ Beliefs walk   ____ Mentoring walk
_X_ Vision walk   ____ Curricular walk
____ Standards walk   ____ Maintenance walk
____ Teaming walk   ____ Addressing individual concern
____ Classroom management walk   ____ New instructional initiative walk

Reflections: *When I read your weekly parent newsletter, I noticed that you had the school's vision statement printed on it. Mrs. Keck, that is a wonderful idea that I will definitely share with the entire staff. We talk so much about making our vision a living document and you have made that a reality. If we believe that we ensure the success of every child, then we should continue to steward that vision through all of our actions. Thank you for all that you do to not only steward our vision, but to also model best practices for students and staff.*

OBSTACLES AND KEYS

One of the obstacles that many school leaders face is time. Leaders may feel that they do not have time during a busy day to be interactive in their buildings. If leaders believe that they should be more visible within the school community, fitness walks are a way in which they can act on this belief.

The keys to fitness walks are that they provide a time-efficient and informal observation tool to stay connected to the needs of the organization. When leaders exercise fitness walks they obtain a great deal of information to assist them in building and sustaining a successful organization.

LEADERSHIP EXERCISES

The following exercises will assist you in the growth and development of your leadership skills. You will be asked to identify evidence or artifacts that showcase your leadership performance. You are encouraged to utilize these exercises both individually and collectively within your school community.

Exercise 7.1   Fitness Walks

What is a fitness walk? Fitness walks examine how inviting the school appears to its diverse community. They look at strategies that can be employed to make the school more inviting to the families and community. Fitness walks provide opportunities for parent involvement. They also allow opportunities to improve instructional techniques and curriculum implementation.

Who might benefit: principal, assistant principal team leader, teacher, special education teacher, student teacher, parent, community members, and so on.

PURPOSES FOR A FITNESS WALK

_____ Student(s) observation   _____ Classroom event

_____ Classroom management   _____ New instructional initiative

_____ Curriculum implementation   _____ Daily contacts

_____ School culture   _____ Maintenance issues

_____ Safe environment   _____ Addressing individual needs

FITNESS WALK PROTOCOL

1. Identify the purpose(s) of a fitness walk.
2. Discuss the purpose with classroom teachers whose classrooms you would visit.
3. Develop a method for taking notes during the fitness walk.
4. Write up your observations as soon as possible following the fitness walk.

    a. What did you learn from the fitness walk?

_____

_____

_____

_____

_____

    b. How will the knowledge that you gained from the fitness walk benefit the organization?

_____

_____

_____

_____

_____

    c. How will you disseminate this information to other members of the school community?

_____

_____

_____

_____

_____

Exercise 7.2   Fitness Walk Postcard

The following feedback postcard can be utilized by the leader or a team that conducts a fitness walk.

Name: _____

Date: _____

Purpose for a walk-through:

_____ TL fitness walk   _____ Culture walk
_____ Beliefs walk   _____ Mentoring walk
_____ Vision walk   _____ Curricular walk
_____ Standards walk   _____ Maintenance walk
_____ Teaming walk   _____ Addressing individual concern
_____ Classroom management walk   _____ New instructional initiative walk

Reflections:

_____

_____

_____

Exercise 7.3   Artifact

Identify artifacts or evidence of your visible presence or fitness walks. Locate or create an artifact to place in your leadership journey album. One artifact may be a completed fitness walk postcard. Other artifacts school leaders have identified are pictures or video recordings of reading the walls, or copies of data that was collected during a fitness walk. Take a minute to jot down a few of your leadership visibility artifacts that will be placed in your journey album.

_____
_____
_____
_____
_____
_____

Exercise 7.4   Reflective Practice

What is the focus of your first fitness walk? How will you share this information with your staff to assist them in using fitness walks?

_____
_____
_____
_____
_____
_____
_____
_____
_____
_____

Dear Diary,

As a first year principal I searched for many ways to increase my visible presence. I had a professional goal to watch, learn, and participate in my first year. By getting out into the building every day I learned a great deal about the members of the community, the physical environment, and the curriculum. We had many district changes that were occurring, and it was so important for me to gauge the climate of the school.

When I read a few articles on learning walks I thought that I should find some way to use some of the ideas. The term learning walk *worked for me at the time, because that is what I was doing. I enjoyed learning through these walks, but I also knew that I was increasing my fitness as a leader. Thus the term* fitness walk *was created.*

I continue to use fitness walks and am always searching for new ways to introduce this method to all members of the school community. I still feel like there is never enough time, but I realize that the benefits of fitness walks far outweigh the time that is required.

Kellie

RESOURCES

Barnes, F., & M. Miller (2001, April). Data Analysis by Walking Around. *AASA Web Publications, 58*(4), 20–26.

Connors, N. (2000). *If You Don't Feed the Teachers They Eat the Students: Guide to Success for Administrators and Teachers.* Nashville, Tenn.: Incentive.

Covey, S., A. R. Merrill, & R. R. Merrill. (1994). *First Things First.* New York: Simon and Schuster.

Downey, C., B. Steffy, F. English, L. Frase, & W. Poston (2004). *The Three-Minute Classroom Walk-Through: Changing School Supervisory Practice One Teacher at a Time.* Thousand Oaks, CA: Corwin.

Dyer, W. (2004). *The Power of Intention: Learning to Co-create Your World Your Way.* Carlsbad, Calif.: Hay House.

Ginsberg, M., & D. Murphy (2002, May). How Walkthroughs Open Doors. *Educational Leadership.*

Kouzes, J., & B. Posner (1999). *Encouraging the Heart: A Leader's Guide to Rewarding and Recognizing Others.* San Francisco: Jossey-Bass.

Richardson, J. (2001, October/November). Seeing through New Eyes. *Tools for Schools.*

Resnick, L. (1995). From Aptitude to Effort: A New Foundation for Our Schools. *Daedalus, 11*(4), 55–62.

Robbins, P., & H. Alvy (1995). *The Principal's Companion: Strategies and Hints to Make the Job Easier.* Thousand Oaks, Calif.: Corwin.

8

MENTORING: FINDING A TRAVEL COMPANION

This dance of mentoring and learning stimulates self-expansion. When we need to learn, we become open to receiving; once we have learned, we immediately become open to giving.

—Huang & Lynch, 1995, 7

LEADERSHIP QUALITIES: RECIPROCAL, PASSION, AND TRUST

Guiding Questions

How will a mentoring relationship assist you in your growth as a learner?
In what ways will mentoring build leadership capacity?
How can mentoring benefit the entire school community?

Transformational Leadership Fitness Areas

4 Provides individualized support
5 Provides intellectual stimulation for professional growth

SIGHTS TO SEE

This chapter will provide a mentoring model that provides ways to build relationships, increase leadership capacity, and maximize organizational learning. Mentors play a variety of roles. Traditional mentoring programs often require mentors to be an experts or gurus, thus establishing mentor/protégé relationships. Roles such as wizard, motivator, or sergeant can impede learning as well as relationship building (Bell 1996). Our model of collaborative leadership is based on mentors as partners. In this approach the partner's relationship is based on learning: "You are responsible for your own learning. I am responsible for supporting, facilitating, and learning with you" (Bell 1996, 24).

School leaders should seek out a learning partner as a mentor during their leadership journey.

This partner may provide both guidance and support to build a strong foundation for a mentoring relationship. Effective mentoring begins with building relationships based on trust and shared values. Once the relationship is established there are reciprocal benefits for both partners. This chapter will focus on ways that these relationships can be built and learning can be enhanced for both the individuals as well as the organization. "Leadership in Action" provides a mentoring experience that features elementary through graduate students as learning partners.

TRADITIONAL MENTORING PROGRAMS

Many traditional mentoring programs were designed to meet state requirements for school reform. As a result, many districts have failed to see the potential of mentoring relationships. Mentoring pairs have traditionally been preassigned; neither the mentor nor the mentee were involved in the choice of partner. These pairings may be likened to prearranged marriages. As with a prearranged marriage, two strangers are joined together with limited or no input from themselves. Neither person may be aware of the other's beliefs, qualities, or similarities. It is simply assumed that these relationships will be successful. Too often mentors and mentees have little in common yet are expected to work together toward organizational norms. Existing mentoring programs continue to fall short due to lack of training, relationship building, resources, and time.

Mentoring relationships should not be limited to new teachers. Organizational leaders may also benefit from effective mentoring relationships. Leaders, like teachers, need to find mentoring partners in order to grow and learn. This mentoring manual can be utilized by anyone within the organization, no matter what role they play.

Historically, mentoring has been a one-way learning experience. Many mentoring programs focus primarily on the mentor as the one with the knowledge and expertise, and the mentee as a sponge who will soak it all up. In a true mentoring relationship learning is reciprocal, a two-way process: "The focus of mentoring . . . has moved from a product-oriented model, characterized by the transfer of knowledge, to a process-oriented relationship involving knowledge acquisition, application, and critical reflection" (Zachary 2000, 4). Have you participated in a mentoring program? How were the partners assigned? What did you find beneficial about this experience? What could have been better about this experience?

_____

_____

_____

_____

_____

THE MENTORING RELATIONSHIP

A model for building, sustaining, and assessing mentoring relationships will be shared within this section. The book *Managers as Mentors* (Bell 1996) states, "Mentoring is an honor. Except for love, there is no greater gift one can give another than the gift of growth. It is a rare privilege to help another learn, have the relevant wisdom useful to another, and have someone who can benefit from that wisdom" (12). Many mentoring pairings can exist within a school environment: teacher-student, cooperating teacher-student teacher, coach-player, principal-teacher, superintendent-principal, team leader-teacher, department head-teacher, and so on. The next steps will provide a model for building, sustaining, and accessing successful mentoring relationships.

Building Mentoring Relationships

The first step to building a mentoring relationship is to determine how mentor pairs will be established. A school leader may invite everyone within the organization to complete an inventory, like the one found at the end of this chapter. This mentoring inventory will provide information that may indicate compatibility.

Some compatible mentoring partners are found without the use of a formal inventory. We may informally discover in a colleague values, interests, and experiences that are similar to our own. We may discover a colleague as a mentor through a working relationship. These shared values may be the foundation for a mentoring relationship. Some questions that you may want to ask yourself before beginning a mentoring relationship are, How will I grow as a result of spending time with this person? How would our school be strengthened as a result of this mentoring relationship? How would students benefit from this mentoring relationship? Identify a colleague with whom you would like to develop a mentoring relationship. How would you respond to some of the previous questions? Consider how you might initiate a mentoring partnership with this person.

_____

_____

_____

_____

_____

Parker Palmer states in _The Courage to Teach_ (1998), "Good teaching is an act of hospitality toward the young, and hospitality is always an act that benefits the host even more than the guest. . . . In ancient nomadic cultures, the food and shelter one gave to a stranger yesterday is the food and shelter one hopes to receive from the stranger tomorrow. . . . By offering hospitality, one participates in the endless weaving of a social fabric on which all can depend. Thus, the gift of sustenance for the guest, becomes a gift of hope for the host" (50). A mentoring relationship may have many purposes, but the common denominator is reciprocal learning. Reciprocal learning occurs when both partners are able to fulfill the role of teacher and student.

Guiding principles should be established to build the mentoring relationship. York-Barr, Sommers, Ghere, and Montie (2001) provide a few examples of guiding principles in mentoring relationships: be present, be open, listen without judgment and with empathy, seek understanding, view learning as mutual, honor the person, and honor the process (25). The mentoring partners should identify and record their guiding principles. These should serve as a reminder of the commitments the partners have made to one another.

Another key element of building a mentoring relationship is to establish goals for the mentoring process. Strong mentor partners should set both individual and mutual goals. "Reflective practitioners are educators who are active learners, who know their values and beliefs, and who regularly set learning goals for themselves" (Kelleher 2002, 20). Goals that mentoring partners may wish to focus on are developing and implementing strategies for classroom or school management; planning and organizing curriculum; assessing and evaluating teachers or students; creating techniques to increase parental and community involvement; adjusting to new roles and responsibilities; and receiving support both mentally and emotionally.

Sustaining Mentoring Relationships

A *mentor agreement* documents the facts that a relationship exists and that each member is making a commitment to learn. This agreement certifies that both partners have agreed to support one another as leaders and learners within the school community. Partners who feel that they are not growing from mentoring arrangements should revisit their goals and modify them as needed. Mentor partners may wish to use the mentoring agreement that is provided at the end of the chapter, or they may create their own.

Time is a gift that we give to one another to sustain a mentoring partnership.

> If we want to support each other's inner lives, we must remember a simple truth: the human soul does not want to be fixed, it wants simply to be seen and heard. If we want to see and hear a person's soul, there is another truth we must remember: the soul is like a wild animal—tough, resilient, and yet shy. When we go crashing through the woods shouting for it to come out so we can help it, the soul will stay in hiding. But if we are willing to sit quietly and wait for a while, the soul may show itself. (Palmer 1998, 151)

It is the time and conversation that partners extend to one another that allow the human soul to show itself. Reflective practice becomes another gift that partners offer to one another.

Assessing Mentoring Relationships

Within a mentoring relationship, the partners assess the relationships through a variety of reflective practices. Reflection is an ongoing process and can be accomplished by using multiple mediums, such as discussion, journaling, and mental processing. "Joining with another person in the process of reflection can result in greater insight about one's practice, especially when trust is high, and the right combination of support and challenge is present" (York-Barr et al. 2001, 13). Guiding questions can be a reflective practice to assess mentoring: How is this relationship benefiting my personal learning? How is this relationship benefiting my partner's learning? How is this relationship supporting the school's vision and success? How is this relationship benefiting students? The answers to these questions maintain the primary focus of the mentoring relationship.

As a result of mentoring, each person increases his or her own capacity for leadership. *Mentoring: The TAO of Giving and Receiving Wisdom* (Huang & Lynch 1995) states that mentoring is "a two-way circular dance that provides opportunities for us to experience both giving and receiving without limitations and fears. . . . This mentor dance celebrates unusually gratifying unions of kindred spirits in soulful relationships" (xii). When mentoring partners form an unlimited union of giving and receiving, they are building leadership capacity within the school community. This increased leadership capacity, in turn, will contribute to an effective school culture.

WHAT ARE THE BENEFITS TO THE ORGANIZATION?

The benefits of reciprocal mentoring relationships extend well beyond the partners themselves. The organization will also benefit from strong mentoring relationships. If mentoring partnerships are rooted in learning then the benefits are numerous. When mentor partners support one another in a reciprocal learning relationship, they in essence support a new generation of school leaders. How have your mentoring experiences helped build and sustain leadership within your school?

_____

_____

_____

The organization also benefits from mentoring by building morale and fostering a commitment to increased productivity. As was stated in the culture chapter, it is critical for an organization to support everyone by creating an environment that is welcoming and comfortable. Mentoring builds morale among colleagues by providing an environment in which members are more productive.

Good mentoring relationships have been found to reduce the attrition of staff members, which is a great benefit to the organization. Richard Ingersoll's study finds, "The average yearly turnover rate in education is 13.2 percent as compared to 11 percent in other professions" (Heller 2004, 5). When individuals are invested and empowered within the school community the turnover rate is diminished. Successful mentoring relationships have been instrumental in lowering the number of teachers who leave the field. Individuals who are active and supported by their colleagues are more likely to remain in their present positions.

The organization benefits from mentoring by creating a better working environment for teachers and thus enhances the learning experience for all students. Inspired teachers will create inspired students. When teachers are empowered by strong mentoring relationships, founded in learning, they will inspire students to find their passion for learning. The capacity for success is limitless when learning is supported and encouraged by all members of the community.

LEADERSHIP IN ACTION

What would a mentoring partnership look like if it involved elementary, high school, undergraduate, and graduate students? An undergraduate professor at a liberal arts college considered this question and decided to make this idea a reality. A program was offered for preservice teachers to teach approximately two hundred at-risk students from inner-city schools. The at-risk students ranged in age from elementary through high school. The preservice teachers used this opportunity to apply instructional best practices and implement classroom management strategies. Also, during the summer term a graduate educational leadership class focused on the roles and responsibilities of school leaders.

The undergraduate instructor contacted the graduate instructor and shared her ideas on how to build a multilevel mentoring experience. Both instructors immediately visualized how this idea could become a reality. They agreed to a process for initiating the mentoring experience and determined when and where this event would take place. A breakfast meet and greet seemed like a comfortable environment for all members of this experience.

The mentoring process would be called Coach for a Day and would focus on a learning experience for all students. The undergraduate students' initial role would be to introduce themselves and share their impressions of entering the field of education. These conversations were designed to be informal and free flowing.

The mentoring experience also provided an opportunity for the high school students in the summer program to interact with and supervise the elementary students. While the undergraduate students were involved in their collegial conversations with the graduates, the high school students were supervising and providing activities for the elementary students in the cafeteria.

On the morning of the event, all of the students seemed apprehensive yet excited about what was going to happen. The graduates and undergraduates began their mentoring experience upstairs, while the school-age children remained downstairs in the cafeteria. The mentor pairs upstairs sat at tables of two or four and began their conversations. Conversations seemed to flow freely. An outsider who entered this room would have had no idea that these people had just met. People moved easily from conversation to conversation. Both instructors stood and observed the activity; they were pleasantly surprised at how well it went.

The experience downstairs between the high school and elementary students also went well. The high school students had to utilize the lessons they had learned about teaching and managing behaviors. This experience may not be viewed by most as a mentoring relationship, but both age groups were learning from one another. Learning is the main purpose of mentoring. These students learned lessons in patience, organization, and collaboration.

The undergraduate and graduate professors could see many possibilities in this mentoring experience. Even though this experience was limited to one morning, it provided a foundation to build upon in the future.

OBSTACLES AND KEYS

One primary obstacle to mentoring is the building and sustaining of relationships. People fail to see the benefits of mentoring for the individuals and the organization. Learning and leadership capacity increase when we build and sustain mentoring relationships.

We need to assist new teachers and leaders to find and hone the skills that they already possess. When we all take time to learn from others and share with them our educational skills, we will build leadership capacity that is limitless. The reciprocal benefits of mentoring will impact the entire school community.

LEADERSHIP EXERCISES

The following exercises will assist you in the growth and development of your leadership skills. You will be asked to identify evidence or artifacts that showcase your leadership performance. You are encouraged to utilize these exercises both individually and collectively within your school community.

Exercise 8.1 Mentoring Inventory

Complete the following questions and consider ways that you might share this information with a colleague in order to establish a successful mentoring relationship. Organizational leaders may utilize this information to pair individuals with similar characteristics.

Why did you choose a career in teaching?

_____

_____

Identify three of your strengths.

_____

_____

What is an area in which you would like to improve?

_____

_____

Identify a few of your interests.

_____

_____

Name three of your core beliefs.

_____

_____

Describe how you prioritize tasks that need to be completed.

_____

_____

How would others describe you as a communicator?

_____

_____

Select three adjectives that a colleague would use to describe you.

_____

_____

Identify your goals for the next year. Three years? Five years?

_____

_____

What do you feel you will gain from a mentoring relationship?

_____

_____

Exercise 8.2   Peer Mentoring Agreement

We have agreed to a mentoring partnership for the upcoming school year. We agree to support one another as leaders and learners within the school community. If during the year we feel that we are not growing from this mentoring arrangement, we will revisit our goals and determine whether our mentoring should continue. We believe that a true relationship is the foundation to a successful mentoring experience, and we will find the time necessary to build and sustain our partnership.

We have agreed on the following goals and objectives of the mentoring relationship:

_____
_____
_____
_____
_____

In order to ensure that our relationship is mutually rewarding and successful, we have committed to the following meeting times and ways we will communicate as peer mentors:

_____
_____
_____
_____
_____

As a means to increase our success, we have also agreed to these guiding principles:

_____
_____
_____
_____
_____

Since learning will be the foundation of our relationship, we have discussed the following ways to maximize learning and provide feedback and reflection for one another:

_____
_____
_____
_____
_____

We agree to meet regularly to build a positive relationship and accomplish our goals. We make these commitments as peers and partners until the completion of the school year, when we will assess our learning, mentoring relationship, and alternatives, and decide whether to conclude or continue our commitment to each other as mentors.

_____   _____
Mentor Signature/Date   Mentor Signature/Date

Exercise 8.3   Artifact

Identify artifacts or evidence of your mentoring relationship. Locate or create an artifact to place in your leadership journey album. One artifact may be a mentoring contract. Other artifacts school leaders have identified that illustrate their mentoring experiences have been agendas from mentoring meetings, reflections on book talks, or other professional development opportunities that you both attended. Take a minute to jot down a few of your mentoring artifacts that will be placed in your journey album.

_____

_____

_____

Exercise 8.4   Reflective Practice

How will a mentoring relationship assist me in my growth as a learner? In what ways will a mentoring relationship build leadership capacity? In what ways can mentoring benefit the entire school community? How will students benefit from a mentoring relationship?

_____

_____

_____

_____

_____

Dear Diary,

I wanted to take a few minutes to write about how my mentoring relationship started with Kris. We began our mentoring relationship approximately six years ago. We started working together through a school/university partnership and began to realize that we had a great deal in common. A few commonalities that we observed were our love of middle-level education, a passion for learning and growing, and a goal to empower educators to become more collaborative leaders.

We realized very early on that we shared a vision of what the education process should look like for all stakeholders within schools. We realized that in order to empower students to love learning, educators needed to feel empowered to love learning as well. Kris encouraged me to pursue various career paths, which eventually led me to my principalship—even though I had previously said it would be "a cold day in _____ _ before I would ever be an administrator." Oh, how things change.

Through working within the school partnership we realized that we both had a passion to learn and grow as educators. Kris was also finishing her doctoral degree and shared her experiences with me, and we began to rely on each other's professional opinions as it related to educational issues. Kris provides a great deal of feedback and support for me in my administrative role. Since Kris is so familiar with the role of administrators, she is able to assist me in realizing the obstacles that I will face as well as the keys to move beyond the difficulties.

It is inspiring to have mentoring conversations. The energy that these discussions produce empower us to take action. For example, we attend conferences and then spend hours discussing how we can use this information to assist teachers and administrators

We are continuing to set our expectations high by writing this book as well as presenting at educational conferences across the country. After each presentation we reflect on what went well and what we could improve on for next time. We not only set high expectations for ourselves but we empower our colleagues to take risks and set their own expectations high to impact student success. Our reciprocal relationship has grown and developed so much over the years that sometimes it is difficult to know which one of us is the teacher and which the student.

Kellie

RESOURCES

Huang, A. C., & J. Lynch (1995). *Mentoring: The TAO of Giving and Receiving Wisdom.* San Francisco: HarperSanFrancisco.

Bell, C. (1996). *Managers as Mentors: Building Partnerships for Learning.* San Francisco: Berrett-Koehler.

Heller, D. (2004). *Teachers Wanted: Attracting and Retaining Good Teachers.* Alexandria, Va.: ASCD.

Kelleher, J. (2000, October). Encouraging Reflective Practice. *Principal Leadership,* 3(2), 20–23.

Maxwell, J. (1995). *Developing the Leaders around You: How to Help Others Reach Their Full Potential.* Nashville, Tenn.: Thomas Nelson.

Palmer, P. (1998). *The Courage to Teach.* San Francisco: Jossey-Bass.

York-Barr, J., W. Sommers, G. Ghere, & J. Montie (2001). *Reflective Practice to Improve Schools: An Action Guide for Educators.* Thousand Oaks, Calif.: Corwin.

Zachary, L. (2000). *The Mentor's Guide: Facilitating Effective Learning Relationships.* San Francisco: Jossey-Bass.

PART 3

REFLECTING ON THE JOURNEY

PORTFOLIOS: A REFLECTION OF OUR LEADERSHIP JOURNEY

A school portfolio is like a garden—It takes planning and hard work, requires the weeding out of unnecessary elements, and promotes positive feelings. You're proud to show it off.

—Bernhardt 2002, 2

LEADERSHIP QUALITIES: REFLECTIVE, ENGAGING, AND COMMUNICATIVE

Guiding Questions

What is the purpose of portfolios?
What is the process for developing a portfolio?
How can a portfolio benefit an individual, team, or organization?

Transformational Leadership Fitness Areas

1 Provides a shared vision and goals
2 Models behavior and best practices
5 Provides intellectual stimulation for professional growth

SIGHTS TO SEE

The portfolio, like a map for a traveler, is a visual guide of where we have been, where we are, and where we are going. The portfolio is evidence of our journey, like a travel album that holds a collection of memories and keepsakes of our most valued experiences. Without a means to capture them, the memories of a journey can quickly be lost in a myriad of busy schedules and new experiences. This chapter will define the purpose, process, and product of a leadership portfolio. It will also identify the benefits for the development of individual, team, department, and schoolwide portfolios. The exercises within this chapter will ask each reader to select a portfolio purpose and framework. The "Leadership in Action" section, unlike those of previous chapters, which highlighted accomplishments and outcomes of other leaders, will feature your own leadership in action. You will compile your own artifacts of leadership experiences and accomplishments to create your leadership journey album.

WHY PORTFOLIOS?

Portfolios provide a means to identify, document, and assess our experiences and accomplishments. The use of portfolios has gained interest and popularity across a wide spectrum in the field of education: preservice training and performance assessment, teacher induction programs, and teacher national board certification. However, portfolios have been less well established for school leaders. Portfolios for leaders may be used to document leadership development and accomplishments. They can also be used to document the development and achievement of the goals of a grade level, department, or team. Another purpose may be a school portfolio of teaching, learning, and leadership artifacts to assess specific goals of the school.

A portfolio is a systematic collection of artifacts that can serve as evidence of the following: professional growth, performance assessment, a showcase of best work, and reflective practice. Administrative leadership programs have increased the utilization of the portfolio as a means to assess growth, knowledge, and performance in ways that lead to administrative certification and licensing. The administrative candidate's portfolio initially may be used as a growth portfolio. By the conclusion of the program the portfolio may also be a means of assessment. Ultimately, this portfolio becomes an interview tool, a way to showcase one's best work; the practicing leader or teacher may wish to use a showcase portfolio for job changes or career advancement. Lastly, and in some cases most importantly, the portfolio process provides leaders with a means for reflective practice and self-assessment.

One principal describes the portfolio process in this way:

> A portfolio is an engine of reflection. It performs as mirrors do in the physical world. The reflections it creates are in the world of ideas, attitudes, and beliefs. Mirrors reflect what is, honestly and straightforward. They can be positioned to give us a different perspective. They focus light in microscopes to allow us careful examination of our work. In reflecting telescopes, mirrors put us in touch with events that are distant from us in space and time. The mirrors of portfolios, when given proper attention and care, allow us to see around the corners of change. (Martin-Kniep 1999, 17)

A portfolio can be a visual depiction of your professional growth, experiences, and accomplishments. A professional portfolio is a visual collection of evidence of successes, challenges, decisions, and influential people in a leader's journey. Describe how you might benefit from the use of a professional portfolio. Consider how it might benefit your growth and development, career advancement, and reflective practice:

_____

_____

_____

THE PORTFOLIO PROCESS

Begin the portfolio process by determining a clear purpose and a suitable framework. Many educators describe portfolio development as one of their most valuable yet challenging experiences. One graduate student considers her portfolio development as the greatest gift she could have given herself. Still another teacher-leader indicates that her portfolio became a mirror in which she could better see her own leadership capacity. A clear purpose and framework is critical for the educator who wishes to develop a portfolio. A lead teacher may develop a portfolio for national board certification, while an assistant principal may create a showcase of best work in order to advance to a principalship. The purpose of a school portfolio may be to address school vision, achievement, the school improvement process, or the diverse needs of the organization. A school portfolio may be used to highlight data collected in support of the federal No Child Left Behind Act. The portfolio purpose will determine the framework or structure to collect and organize evidence or artifacts.

The second step of the portfolio process is to determine a suitable framework. The following are suggestions arising from existing standards or models that can serve as frameworks for portfolio development. They can be modified to suit the purposes and goals of an individual, team, or school portfolio.

The National Board for Professional Teaching Standards

The National Board for Professional Teaching Standards provides a model for lead teachers and future school leaders. Some suggest that the NBPTS provides a new definition of excellence for teaching and is shaping reforms that ensure professional accountability in the teaching profession. Candidates in any content area seeking certification are required to describe, analyze, explain, and reflect on their performance and design portfolios reflective of best teaching practices. The NBPTS offers a standards-based framework of content, theory to practice, and propositions as a foundation to portfolio development. It seeks to identify and recognize teachers who effectively enhance student learning and demonstrate the high level of knowledge, skills, abilities and commitments reflected in the following five core propositions:

- Teachers are committed to students and their learning.
- Teachers know the subjects they teach and how to teach those subjects to students.
- Teachers are responsible for managing and monitoring student learning.
- Teachers think systematically about their practice and learn from experience.
- Teachers are members of learning communities. ("Portfolio Instructions," 2004)

Specific guidelines and content standards for all areas of school personnel can be found at the website for the National Board for Professional Teaching Standards, www.nbpts.org.

Interstate Licensure Consortium and the Council of Chief Officers (ISLLC)

Educational leaders need not look far to find leadership standards that can be used as a framework for portfolios. The ISLLC standards for school leaders were described in chapter 5. Many administrative leadership programs use the standards as a portfolio framework to identify leadership knowledge, dispositions, and skills. Successful leaders model and demonstrate leadership standards in their beliefs, actions, and performance. Each of the ISLLC leadership standards begins with a focus on student learning and success, stating this ideal: "A school administrator is an educational leader who promotes the success of all students" (Wilmore 2002, 13). The standards seek to shape the development of a vision, learning culture, a safe environment, partnerships, ethics and values, and a political environment where best practices are enhanced and fostered.

Many aspiring school leaders begin collecting evidence using the six ISLLC leadership standards as a framework. Consider possible artifacts you might already have that show evidence of Standard 2: "A school administrator is an educational leader who promotes the success of all students by advocating, nurturing, and sustaining a school culture and instructional program conducive to student learning and staff professional growth." Possible artifact(s):

The School Portfolio Toolkit: A Comprehensive Framework for School Improvement

Victoria Bernhardt (2002) has created a resource that serves as a framework for school improvement and portfolio development. A school portfolio organized using this framework would include these areas: information and analysis, student achievement, quality planning, professional development, leadership, partnership development, and continuous improvement and evaluation. "The School Portfolio Toolkit was written to support school personnel with the mechanics of putting together a school portfolio as well as offer processes and strategies to move whole school staffs into and through continuous school improvement" (Bernhardt 2002, 5). The resources listed at the end of this chapter provide many alternatives for schools to use in the development of a school portfolio.

Components of a Principal's Portfolio

Still another potential framework for a school principal is *The Principal Portfolio* (1997), by Genevieve Brown and Beverly Irby. This resource provides a framework of the key components of a principal's portfolio. This framework includes the following:

- An introduction
- A résumé or vita
- A leadership framework, which includes a philosophy of education, philosophy of leadership, vision for learners, vision for teachers, vision for the organization, vision for professional growth, and method of vision attainment
- Five-year goals
- Learner-centered leadership
- Curriculum and instruction
- Effective communication
- Building a learning community
- Fiscal accountability
- Accolades

The Principal Portfolio (1997) is "a resource that holds great potential. It provides authentic documentation of the complicated and situational work of principals on their campuses, and it promotes self-assessment and reflection essential for improving practice and transforming schools" (viii). In addition to the framework provided, Brown and Irby offer many suggestions on the practical and reflective development of a principal's portfolio.

Teaming Portfolio

The development of a team portfolio would be well suited to the framework suggested by John Arnold and Chris Stevenson (1998). As a team progresses toward creating a team mission, vision, and beliefs, the portfolio becomes a natural place to showcase its development. In our work with teams the Stevenson and Arnold framework has provided a means of professional development and assessment for teaming. The following characteristics are recommended as a framework for a teaming portfolio. They address team vision and philosophy:

- What do we believe? What are our values?
- Team governance: What are team roles and responsibilities? How do we make decisions as a team? What role do students play in team governance?
- Procedures: How do we function as a team?
- Team identity: Who are we? What do we stand for? How do we recognize our successes?
- Communication: How do we keep team members and others informed?
- Curriculum: What and how do we learn?
- Accountability: How do we measure and assess what is being accomplished?
- Teacher efficacy: What are the personal benefits of teaming for me?

Taking the First Step

The frameworks suggested in this chapter are just a few ideas of how portfolios can be structured. Other possible starting frameworks may be the ten essentials of collaborative leadership or the six features of transformational leadership. The framework of a "professional learning community" in chapter 6 is still another option for a schoolwide approach to mapping the past, present, and future of a school community. Most important is to select an initial framework and make a commitment to getting started.

Fundamental to starting any journey is taking the first step: "A journey of a thousand miles must begin with a single step." When asked what was most difficult about developing a portfolio, teachers in graduate programs for leadership cited getting started. Determining a framework is the first step on the portfolio development journey. What framework will you chose for your portfolio?

THE PORTFOLIO AS A PRODUCT: ORGANIZING AND DESIGNING

In this segment you will learn specific steps in how to design evidence that supports the purpose of your portfolio. Victoria Bernhardt (2002) suggests that "the school portfolio is like a photograph album—It brings back memories for the people involved, shows changes over time, and introduces people to thinking in ways they have never thought before" (2). While the purpose and process segments include technical decisions, such as the selection of a framework, the next segment will invite each traveler to consider unique and artistic ways to visualize and assemble a journey album. This becomes an opportunity for self-reflection, discovery, and a celebration of achievements over time.

How to *DESIGN* a Portfolio

The following are six steps that will help you to design your portfolio:

1. *D*etermine a design
2. Collect *E*vidence
3. *S*ystematically arrange
4. *I*dentify what is important
5. *G*raphically enhance it
6. *N*ever stop developing

Step 1: Design Your Portfolio   Design your portfolio in a way that best reflects you. You will need to purchase a few items as you begin this phase of designing your portfolio. You will need a three-ring binder, dividers, tabs, plastic cover sheets, and folders. The collection and development of artifacts to design your portfolio begins with identifying significant events, people, and accomplishments. This can be challenging if you have not previously attempted to chronicle these areas of your life. Complete the following six activities as a means to identify some of your key artifacts. This can be more successful and enjoyable when done with some of the people who have been part of these events.

Figure 9.1   Chronological Timeline

Identify and sequence key dates and events of a selected year. Feel free to create additional timelines for each year.

<-->

Event/Year/Months

Significant events

Highlight or circle the most significant events on your timeline above. You will want to show evidence of these significant events in your portfolio.

Figure 9.2   Influential People

Who are five key people who were influential in the events of your timeline(s). Record the name of each in the circles below.

Figure 9.3   Actions and Achievements

Review the influential people and significant events of your timeline(s). What are five achievements of which you are most proud?

1. _____
2. _____
3. _____
4. _____
5. _____

Figure 9.4   Obstacles

Identify four areas or obstacles that have posed challenges for you in your achievements and significant events. What actions have you taken to overcome these challenges?

1. _____
2. _____
3. _____
4. _____

Figure 9.5   What Leadership Qualities Do I Possess?

Circle the qualities that best describe your leadership relative to the significant achievements and actions of your timeline(s). For example, earning a master's degree in educational leadership may have been a significant achievement. The following qualities have been highlighted at the beginning of each chapter. Feel free to identify additional leadership qualities and add to the list below.

Leadership Qualities

Courage	*Communication*	*Commitment*
Risk Taking	*Empowerment*	*Inspiration*
Hope	*Collaboration*	*Accountability*
Visionary	*Creative*	*Discerning*
Servanthood	*Relationship Manager*	*Teamwork*
Modeling	*Reciprocal*	*Passion*
Trust	*Perseverance*	*Problem Solving*
Generosity	*Supportive*	*Grateful*
Caring	*Self-Discipline*	

Step 2: Gather Evidence as Artifacts   Now that you have identified main events, achievements, and people, you will need to start to collect the actual evidence or artifacts to place into your portfolio. As in an archeological dig, you will locate some of your artifacts easily preserved at the surface, while others will require more intense searching and digging. Some of your most significant events and achievements may not have existing artifacts. In these cases you will need to design an artifact that best illustrates the experience you would like to preserve for your portfolio. Review the following three artifact lists (Figure 9.6). Add additional artifacts from the previous activities or reflections you have generated so far. Place a check mark by the ones that you believe will be artifacts for your portfolio. Begin to collect and place in a file artifacts that you would like to consider for your portfolio.

Step 3: Systematically Place Artifacts in Your Framework   As you begin to review your file of artifacts, you will need to determine how each artifact fits into the purpose and framework of your portfolio. Place each artifact in a clear cover sheet. Categorize and place your artifacts in a binder, in the most appropriate section of your framework. For example, if you have selected the ISLLC standards as your framework, place your vision statement in section 1, "Building a Shared Vision."

Figure 9.6 Depths of Artifacts

ON THE SURFACE

_____Résumé
_____Reference letters
_____Annual performance review
_____Products of committee work: meeting agendas, curriculum development, or outcomes
_____Evidence of student learning (curriculum results, test scores, data collection, assessments from teachers, student work samples)
_____Products of school safety/discipline efforts toward a positive learning environment
_____Professional development: training, conferences, and classes
_____Communication/correspondence with parents, teachers, and community members
_____School improvement plan: participation and development
_____Technology applications and proficiency
_____Other

POSSIBLE ARTIFACTS BELOW THE SURFACE

_____Personal goals
_____Roles and responsibilities outside the classroom: team leader, athletic coach, department head, activity supervisor/coordinator
_____Professional books read
_____Involvement in student activities and school events
_____Interactions with parents with an emphasis on parents as partners
_____Staff mentoring, collaboration, and teaming efforts
_____Staff presentations, handouts, or professional in-services
_____Other

OTHER POSSIBLE ARTIFACTS: DIGGING DEEPER

_____Personal vision and mission statement
_____Personal and professional beliefs
_____Leadership strengths, capacity, and qualities
_____Leadership standards knowledge, application, and skills
_____Evidence of improvement and growth over time
_____Evidence of the ability to solve problems
_____Other

Step 4: Identify the Importance of Each Artifact   Identifying the importance of each artifact is a critical step to telling your story. Write a brief description or reflection for each artifact that is not self-explanatory. For example, when you return home from traveling, photos and souvenirs have exceptional meaning and value to you. However, without a description or captions, another person will not understand their purpose or value. A note, caption, or reflection can be added to each artifact to clarify its meaning and purpose.

Step 5: Graphic and Visual Enhancement   Once artifacts have been assembled into a notebook, many graphic options are possible. Thematic paper can be used to display and artistically enhance each artifact. Photos, quotes, and visual displays of personal experiences add to each portfolio's unique story. Artwork or clip art can also enhance the appearance of the portfolio. A well-organized table of contents, an introductory page and purpose, and an artistic cover make each portfolio as valuable as if it were a work of art.

Step 6: Never Stop Improving and Collecting Evidence   The development of a portfolio is a dynamic and fluid process. Like the person that creates it, the portfolio is always evolving and never finished. As leaders we go through phases in our careers, and portfolios will be among the products of each phase. As for the school or person that the portfolio reflects, growth and change is continuous. Consequently, the self-portrait is never finished.

OBSTACLES AND KEYS

Portfolio development provides an opportunity for documenting growth and achievements as an individual, team, or school community. The challenge in developing a portfolio is the personal time commitment required to truly reflect on who we are as human beings. The authentic portfolio requires time, reflection, and continuous learning.

This chapter was designed to explain for school leaders the purpose, process, and product of portfolio development. The portfolio process is not intended to be an isolated or lonely one. It is an engaging and interactive experience that should be shared and celebrated with others. The portfolio provides a way to showcase artifacts, share experiences, and celebrate a self-portrait of leadership.

LEADERSHIP EXERCISES

The following exercises will assist you in the growth and development of your leadership skills. You will be asked to identify evidence or artifacts that showcase your leadership performance. You are encouraged to utilize these exercises both individually and collectively within your school community.

Exercise 9.1   Portfolio Bingo

PURPOSE

- To identify the range and diversity of leaders' portfolio artifacts
- To publicly share and acknowledge individual artifacts and their contextual significance
- To enhance individual reflection and leadership growth through the development of leadership artifacts

Participants will receive a bingo card and will earn marks on each space that is called that corresponds with one of their portfolio artifacts. One person will be the caller for bingo and will draw and announce artifact categories that correspond with the bingo cards. Participants will mark their bingo card each time an artifact category is drawn and it is an artifact they have established in their portfolio. Once a participant has five artifacts in a row, they have bingo. Once they have bingo, they will share their corresponding artifacts with the rest of the participants. This can be repeated numerous times depending on available time.

B	I	N	G	O
Leadership Beliefs	Knowledge of Leadership Theory or Models	Letters of Reference	Students with Special Needs Knowledge or Experience	Knowledge of Leadership Standards
An Example of Collaborative Leadership	Staff Development Training	Awards or Achievements	Community Awareness or Experience	Job Performance Evaluations
Notes, Letters, and Feedback	Table of Contents	Résumé	Graphics or Symbols of Leadership	A Mission or Vision Statement
Introduction	Notebook or Binder Cover/Title	Professional Goals	Fulfilling a Leadership Role beyond the School Day	Communication Artifact
Evidence of Growth or Improvement	A Theme or Pattern of Leadership	Leadership Strengths and Qualities	Representative Leadership Photos	Evidence of Technology Proficiency

DEBRIEFING: BINGO REFLECTIONS AND OBSERVATIONS

Answer the following questions at the conclusion of the bingo activity:

1. How did each participant determine if the artifact qualifies for the category drawn?
2. How does this activity enhance the understanding participants have of their own leadership?
3. How does this activity improve the development of portfolios from an experience of isolation to a collective or community based experienced?

Exercise 9.2   Portfolio Reflection

Reflect back on your artifacts from this and the previous chapters of this book, and look ahead to those of the next and last chapter. Circle the exercises below where you have initiated an artifact or reflective response. What did you learn about yourself through your artifacts and responses to each activity? How can these responses be developed into artifacts for your portfolio?

THE TEN ESSENTIALS EXERCISE LIST

Introduction

- Leadership Self-Profile

Chapter 1: Transformational Leadership (TL)

- TL Fitness Program Self Assessment
- TL Fitness Plan
- Artifact
- Reflection

Chapter 2: Beliefs

- Raising the BAR
- Beliefs and Vision Worksheet
- Artifact
- Reflection

Chapter 3: Vision and Mission

- Painting Our Vision: The Ideal Day
- Beliefs and Vision Worksheet
- Artifact
- Reflection

Chapter 4: Standards

- Leadership Fitness Inventory
- Fitness Leadership Plan
- Leadership Standards in Action
- Artifact
- Reflection

Chapter 5: Teaming

- Four-Square Activity
- Artifact
- Reflection

Chapter 6: Culture

- Conducting an Archeological Search for Culture
- The Language and Culture of Music

- Southwest Airlines Culture and Community
- Artifact
- Reflection

Chapter 7: Visibility

- Fitness Walks
- Fitness Walk Postcard
- Artifact
- Reflection

Chapter 8: Mentoring

- Mentoring Inventory
- Peer Mentoring Agreement
- Artifact
- Reflection

Chapter 9: Portfolios

- Portfolio Bingo
- Portfolio Reflection
- Leadership in Action

Chapter 10: Celebrating Success

- Celebrating the Ten Essentials
- Most Valuable Person
- Team Fish Tales
- Reflection

Exercise 9.3   Leadership in Action: Collecting and Assessing Artifacts

This exercise encourages you to grow and strengthen your leadership best practices by assessing some of the artifacts that you have identified at the end of each chapter. Select artifacts from each of the ten essentials chapters. Identify the artifact and place it under the category that best describes its strength. You may wish to place more than one artifact under each essential.

Leadership in Action

Ten Essentials	Emerging The leader has an awareness of the essential and can show minimal evidence that demonstrates some understanding and knowledge	Proficient The leader provides an artifact that clearly demonstrates a thorough understanding and knowledge of the essential	Exemplary The leader provides artifacts and evidence that showcase understanding, knowledge, and leadership actions for each essential
Transformational Leadership			
Leadership Beliefs			
Personal or Shared Vision and Mission			
Standards			
Teaming			
Culture			

Visible Presence

Mentoring

Leadership Portfolio

Celebrating and Recognizing Success

Dear Diary,

I have taught portfolio development to many students, teachers, and leaders. My portfolio knowledge comes from my own experience. It began around a dining room table with piles of "stuff" with my two good friends Barb and Debbie. The three of us were considering career moves—and realized we needed portfolios. And like many leaders, we just figured it out on our own. A year after I left my principalship and was teaching in higher education, I received one of my most prized portfolio artifacts. It has not only held a sacred spot in my portfolio but also occupied a prominent place in the introduction of my dissertation. Here it is:

> *A strong, passionate principal can change a school from a good school to an excellent school. The principal can be the key to an enthusiastic staff and willing students. A principal can encourage teachers to start great programs and projects that get the students involved. She can challenge the staff and students by having high expectations and addressing the important school rules. A strong principal isn't afraid to take risks and get the middle school involved in the community and other impressive projects. A passionate principal will make the staff want to work hard to please her, so they are more likely to be more creative and energetic toward the students. This will make the students more involved. On the other hand, if a principal stays hidden and isn't very involved in the school, the staff will not be very motivated by her expectations. It will have a negative affect on the student body as well. A principal has the most influence over the entire school.*
> *Stephanie*
> *Fall 1998*

Stephanie was a seventh-grader in my middle school. Her description of me as a principal was the most valuable feedback I could have received. Some artifacts become a gift. This is one I will always treasure.

Kris

RESOURCES

Bernhardt, V. (2002). *The School Portfolio: A Comprehensive Framework for School Improvement.* Larchmont, N.Y.: Eye on Education.

Brown, G., & B. Irby (1997). *The Principal Portfolio.* Thousand Oaks, Calif.: Corwin.

Campbell, D., P. Cignetti, B. Melenyzer, D. Nettles, & R. Wyman (2001). *How to Develop a Professional Portfolio.* Boston: Allyn & Bacon.

Costantino, P., & M. DeLorenzo (2002). *Developing a Professional Teaching Portfolio: A Guide for Success.* Boston: Allyn & Bacon.

Dietz, M. (2001). *Designing the School Leader's Portfolio.* Arlington Heights, Ill.: Skylight.

Green, R. L. (2001). *Practicing the Art of Leadership: A Problem-Based Approach to Implementing the ISLLC Standards.* Columbus, Ohio: Prentice Hall.

Jones, L. (1996). *The Path: Creating Your Mission Statement for Work and for Life.* New York: Hyperion.

Looper, S., and R. Wyatt (1999). *So You Have to Have a Portfolio: A Teacher's Guide to Preparation and Presentation.* Thousand Oaks, Calif.: Corwin.

Martin-Kniep, G. (1999). *Capturing the Wisdom of Practice: Professional Portfolios for Educators.* Alexandria, Va.: ASCD.

Portfolio Instructions. *National Board for Professional Teaching Standards.* Retrieved April 13, 2004, from www.nbpts.org.

Wilmore, E. (2002). *Principal Leadership: Applying the New Educational Leadership Constituent Council (ELCC) Standards.* Thousand Oaks, Calif.:Corwin.

10

CELEBRATING SUCCESS: ENCOURAGING AND RECOGNIZING WHAT IS VALUED

Encouragement comes wrapped in packages of all kinds . . . with a thank you, a story, and a smile. . . . Your imagination is the only limit.

—Kouzes & Posner 1999, 151

LEADERSHIP QUALITIES: PASSION, GENEROSITY, CARING, GRATITUDE, AND SUPPORT.

Guiding Questions

How do you communicate and demonstrate what you value?
How do recognize and celebrate what you value?
What behaviors do you reward?

Transformational Leadership Fitness Areas

2 Models behavior and best practices
4 Provides individualized support
6 Creates high expectations

SIGHTS TO SEE

Celebrations provide opportunities to recognize individual, team, and organizational accomplishments. Most cultures consist of traditions where people gather to commemorate special events with music, food, and recognition. This chapter will identify the importance of celebrations as a way to recognize and celebrate the human spirit. Several frameworks will identify the benefits of recognition and celebration for the organization and its members. When leaders provide time to systematically celebrate and recognize success, they affirm the values of the culture. The transformational leader builds relationships by purposefully noticing and acknowledging those who share in the commitments of the organization.

The final chapter of this leadership guide will encourage each traveler to reflect on and celebrate their travel accomplishments. You have discovered new frameworks, gained new perspectives, and collected evidence of leadership that should be celebrated in your development as a leader. Chapter 10 will describe the purpose of celebrating, ways to individually and collectively recognize success, and provide specific examples of recognition (in the "Leadership in Action" segment).

WHY CELEBRATIONS?

One of the strongest muscles in the human body is the heart. Whether the human body performs or struggles is based on the strength of the heart. Organizations also need a strong heart, and this can be found and developed through cultural celebrations. Celebrations are a cultural expression of events, accomplishments, and people. Music, gifts, and gatherings are traditional expressions of gratitude or appreciation. Celebrations are a way of conveying meaning and reinforcing the values of a group of people. Southwest Airlines expresses the importance of cultural celebrations:

> Without celebration, we are robbed of our life and vitality that energizes the human spirit. Latent and underdeveloped though it might be, there is within our nature as human beings an inherent need to sing, dance, love, laugh, mourn, tell stories, and celebrate. . . . There is no culture in the world that doesn't embrace some form of festivity. To deny our need to celebrate is to deny a part of what it means to be human. . . . When we work in an environment where we are not encouraged to express this festive nature, our celebrative faculties, like unused muscles, begin to atrophy. (Freiberg & Freiberg 1996, 177)

The benefits of celebrating include reinforcement of positive norms, recognition of cultural behaviors, and recognition of individuals (DuFour & Eaker 1998). When leaders recognize the values, behaviors, and people who contribute to the success of the organization, they reinforce for others what is valued. This recognition encourages through modeling, praising, and celebrating. At its most basic level, celebrations provide fun and enjoyment for those committed to the goals and vision of the organization. Give an example of a recent celebration that recognized a colleague, team, or organization. How did this contribute to one of the goals of the organization?

_____

_____

_____

_____

Schools are places where the human spirit can either soar or fail. It is the responsibility of the leader to build a human capacity for hope and gratitude: "This is the fundamental behavioral truth of relationship building. We are drawn to, and return to, that which is rewarding" (Rubin 2002, 27). Personal recognition of a person raises the individual and one's relationship with him or her to a higher level. Personal recognition is also an opportunity for a leader to affirm and remind others what is important in the culture of a school. The transformational leader values human capacity. The greatest way to build this capacity is to individually and collectively celebrate the contributions of its members.

While some leaders find it natural to celebrate individual accomplishments but are less comfortable doing so in a group setting. Richard DuFour and Robert Eaker, in their book *Professional Learning Communities at Work* (1998), indicate that some leaders' efforts at recognition are private, even "surreptitious acknowledgment," in order to avoid awkwardness and any appearance of favoritism (142). Private recognition, however, does not promote cultural change in relationship building, support, or values. When leaders believe that it is their responsibility to recognize the worth of each individual, a variety of creative approaches can be found to publicly celebrate the organization and its members.

FRAMEWORKS FOR CELEBRATING SUCCESS

Three frameworks will be introduced to assist leaders in creating a culture of celebrating success. One framework is *The Seven Essentials of Encouraging the Heart,* by Kouzes and Posner (1999). Another is taken from a lighthearted book by Neila A. Connors, *If You Don't Feed the Teachers They'll Eat the Students* (2000). Still a third popular approach to improve cultural encouragement and recognition is that of *Fish Tales* (Lundin et al. 2002).

The first framework comes from *Encouraging the Heart: A Leaders' Guide to Rewarding and Recognizing Others* (1999). The authors, James Kouzes and Barry Posner, created this followup to an earlier book, *The Five Practices of Exemplary Leadership,* because *encouraging the heart* is one of the most important characteristics of exemplary leadership. *Encouraging the Heart* offers principles and practices essential to collaborative leadership. These components are simplistic truisms that reinforce a leader's opportunity to demonstrate personal and organizational values:

- *Set clear standards:* Organizations must define clear goals as targets for individual and teams to succeed. These goals establish the standards for organizational success and provide a way to recognize people who achieve these standards.
- *Expect the best:* Leaders demonstrate and express a belief in the goodness of people, and consequently, organizations get the best performance in return.
- *Pay attention:* The best leaders "have a special radar that picks up positive signals" because they intentionally seek out the value each person (22).
- *Personalize recognition:* Effective leaders personally acquaint themselves with the members of their organization in order to relate with them in meaningful ways.
- *Tell the story:* Leaders utilize stories as a way to teach and emphasize what is valued.
- *Celebrate together:* Publicly recognizing colleagues builds relationships and organizational culture. Efforts to celebrate with our colleagues "humanizes the values and standards" of each person and the organization (28).
- *Set the example:* Every person, particularly the leader, needs to take the initiative to recognize individual, team, and organizational accomplishments in order to build a culture of support and success.

"Leadership in Action" will illustrate how leaders *encourage the heart.*

Leaders demonstrate a wide range of understanding and comfort levels in recognizing and encouraging others. In her book *If You Don't Feed the Teachers* (2000), Neila Connors uses a menu metaphor to identify ways administrators and teachers can provide encouragement. This resource includes numerous self-assessments that provide indicators of when individuals and organizations should celebrate. This author suggests that "on a daily basis, all walks of life arrive at school hoping they will be safe, fed, and assisted" (12). Consequently, a well-adjusted leader provides an environment where adults feel safe, cared for, and appreciated. In order to provide this environment, a healthy leader must be able to demonstrate the following:

- Ability to care for others
- Desire to be successful and contribute to the success of others
- Ability to handle and relieve stress for themselves and others
- General feeling of good health in mind, body, and spirit
- Thoughtfulness and logic in making decisions that impact others

Consider how well you recently exhibited these five indicators. The transformational leader builds relationships that must be cared for and sustained. This framework reminds you of the importance of building and *feeding* these relationships by taking actions that encourage, support, and recognize others: "When a leader takes the time to communicate, care, collaborate, and feed the staff, amazing results occur" (111). It is important that leaders maintain their own fitness in order to care of others. *If You Don't Feed the Teachers* provides leaders with humorous and straightforward strategies to reduce stress and burnout. Through reciprocal encouragement, a leader and follower provide continuous nourishment to one another.

The third framework began in the heart of Seattle, Washington. The setting is a world-famous fish market. Pike Place Fish Market was purchased as a fish stand in 1965 by John Yokoyama, one of the employees. This fish market became world famous not just for throwing fish but because of the unique ways in which each employee would personally interact within the workplace. This small crew of fishmongers began to playfully interact with customers in a way that caused both to feel a greater sense of worth and satisfaction. This connectedness between fishmongers and customers led Charthouse Learning to create four basic principles of what they had observed there. These four principles are the central focus of three books and numerous videos that are used worldwide to emphasize ways that workplaces can demonstrate encouragement and appreciation. These four principles are: play, make their day, be there, choose your attitude.

Play becomes one of the important elements for a successful organization: "Play is not just an activity; it's a state of mind that brings new energy to the tasks at hand and sparks creative solutions" (Lundin, Christenson, & Paul 2002, 5). We make their day through small acts of kindness within the routine of the workday. Ordinary people who care and provide support for one another are demonstrating the third fish principle, be there. Lastly, if fishmongers can demonstrate the principle *Choose Your Attitude*, certainly we can hope that schools and businesses can do the same. Whether working in a fish market or a school, each person can lighten the load by choosing a positive and enthusiastic attitude.

The fish philosophy that originated at world-famous Pike Place Fish Market has generated a vision of hope and possibilities for thousands of companies. The following is the Charthouse Learning mission:

We, the community of Charthouse Learning, are on a constant journey to discover new sources of wisdom, sometimes in unlikely places, that awaken people to live into their full human potential. To illuminate that wisdom, we create inspiring films and learning resources. We then share these creations to help build a community committed to lifelong learning and stewardship of all that we have been given. We believe that it's possible for a person to impact the way other people experience life. Through our work, we can improve the quality of life for others. We are committed to this belief. It's what we do. ("ChartHouse Learning Mission")

The fish philosophy has provided a simple and yet comprehensive framework by which thousands of schools and businesses have transformed themselves.

LEADERSHIP IN ACTION

The following are categories of recognition and symbols that have been awarded to recognize success. In some cases, you may need to read between the lines to understand the context or circumstances of the recognition. In these cases, you will know only that someone did something that was appreciated.

- *Golden Apple Traveling Trophy:* A golden (or brass) apple is presented to a colleague by a colleague for an exceptional act of good teaching.
- *Gift of Time Certificate:* The administration presents a teacher with a certificate that covers his/her class, supervision, or an assignment in order to give some extra free time.
- Hallelujah Chorus *Celebration:* On the last day of school at dismissal time the *Hallelujah Chorus* is played over the loudspeaker to celebrate the end of a successful year. Much laughter follows. Students and staff are awarded a summer of fun.
- *High Energy Award:* This person brings energy and enthusiasm wherever they go. The award is either the Energizer Bunny or a pack of Energizer batteries.
- *Shared Vision Award:* This person is recognized for exceptional visionary skills. The symbol of a lighthouse can be awarded as a gift or a certificate.
- *Good & Plenty of Leadership Award:* An individual or team who have demonstrated plenty of leadership or increased leadership capacity is presented with a bag of Good & Plenty candy.
- *Making a Difference Recognition:* The story of the starfish (McNally 1990, 38) is presented to recognize someone who is *making a difference* for students, colleagues, or the organization.
- *Taking the Plunge:* This award is presented as a humorous symbol for the person who has "taken the plunge" in a task that has been difficult or challenging. A good example is the teacher who makes the decision to start taking courses in an administrative leadership program. The award—a ribbon decorating a small hand plunger, with the person's name added.
- *Treasured Ideas Award:* This recognition is for the creative person who contributes many great ideas to the team or school. A treasure chest or a bag of *treasured* candy is the perfect gift to symbolize this award.
- *Fun-and-Laughter Award:* A person who has brought fun, enjoyment, and laughter to others is also fun to recognize, especially in the presence of others. Obtain a pair of silly glasses and nose, or something as whimsical, from a local party store as a symbol of the fun this person brings to others.
- *Fishing License:* Invite a team or school to read and implement the philosophies found in *Fish Tales* (Lundin et al. 2002). Award a "fishing license" certificate to recognize the participants.
- *Growing by Leaps and Bounds:* Leaders encourage learning from all areas of an organization. Recognize those who have excelled in *leaps and bounds* as learners. A symbolic gift for this award may be a measuring tape or a frog.
- *Juggling Award:* This award is for the person who is a master at juggling multiple roles and responsibilities. A thank you and a set of three rubber balls says it all.
- *Caring for Others Award:* Those who take care of others may be described as a "lifesavers." This

person is recognized either individually or within a group for his or her care of others. This award may be as simple as a bag of LifeSavers candy.

- *Risk-Taking Award:* Successful people take risks to learn and grow. This award should be issued often and can be a great symbolic reminder through the use of a turtle or lobster. (If you don't remember the lobster story, go back to the introduction.)
- *High Hopes Award:* This award recognizes individuals who display high hopes through their actions for themselves and others. The song "High Hopes" by Frank Sinatra is a lighthearted reminder of the hope others bring to all of us.
- *Navigating the Course Award:* This person demonstrates the commitment to stay on course as a leader and learner. They have set clear standards for themselves and model these standards for others. The symbolic award for this recognition is a compass.
- *Going the Distance for Children:* A pin that features a tennis shoe is rotated to persons who have demonstrate an exceptional commitment to going the distance for children. This award is a great reminder to central office administrators, who are less likely to have personal contact with children every day.

OBSTACLES AND KEYS

Celebrating is one of the most natural human responses. A healthy culture invites everyone to be successful and makes celebration each person's responsibility (Dufour & Eaker 1998). Effective leaders find many inclusive ways to recognize positive behavior of all members of the organization and avoid recognition that may appear restrictive or privileged. Celebrating may be an obstacle if leaders attempt to do this alone. Students, teachers, staff, and administrators can all contribute and benefit from celebrating.

A key to celebrating is to recognize the importance of nourishing individuals in ways that also contribute to the purpose and vision of the organization. When both of these aims are accomplished, the result is top performance in a culture of high expectations.

LEADERSHIP EXERCISES

The following exercises will assist you in the growth and development of your leadership skills. You will be asked to identify evidence or artifacts that showcase your leadership performance. You are encouraged to utilize these exercises both individually and collectively within your school community.

Exercise 10.1   Celebrating the Ten Essentials

Reflect on the ten essentials of collaborative leadership. Identify the essentials that you have most successfully demonstrated. How would you personally celebrate your accomplishments of each essential? How would you celebrate organizational accomplishments? Place each of your responses in the chart below.

Celebrating the Ten Essentials

Ten Essentials	Celebrations of Personal Accomplishments	Celebrations of Organizational Accomplishments
Transformational Leadership		
Leadership Beliefs		
Personal and/or Shared Vision and Mission		
Standards		

Teaming

Culture

Visible Presence

Mentoring

Portfolios

Celebrating

Exercise 10.2   Most Valuable Person

Place the names of a class, team, or members of your organization in a container. Ask each person to draw out the name of a person. One person will record the name each person has drawn. Do not reveal the names to the group. Over a two-week period ask each person to notice what is unique about this person. Write a brief, twenty-five-word tribute as a personal recognition about this peer or colleague. Exchange the tributes with each person either individually or with volunteers who are willing to share their tributes with the group.

Exercise 10.3   Team Fish Tales

Ask teams to determine a team name, symbol, roles, and goals using the *Fish Tales* philosophy. Discuss and apply the four Fish Tales principles:

1. *Play:* Play is not just an activity; play is a state of mind that brings energy and sparks creativity.
2. *Make Their Day:* The world becomes a better place the moment you act on an intention to serve another and in some small way provide a *make their day* gesture.
3. *Be There:* You can multitask, but you need to pay attention and *be there* for others.
4. *Choose Your Attitude:* We each choose our attitudes; Your attitude can be one of the most important things you bring to others.

How can this approach be demonstrated in your school? Determine ways you and your team will apply the *Fish Tales* principles. How will your team recognize one another and the organization using the four principles? Plan to conduct a team celebration at the conclusion of this exercise.

Exercise 10.4   Reflective Practice

How will you celebrate your personal and professional accomplishments? How has this final chapter encouraged you in your development as a leader?

_____
_____
_____
_____
_____
_____
_____

Dear Diary,

Teaching is an act of celebration. As a middle school teacher, I considered each day with students a celebration. I tried to create an engaging environment that invited everyone to get involved and excited about learning. Today as a teacher of teachers, I find myself doing the same sort of things. Music, food, stories, and interaction is built into every learning session. I am not sure if I do it more for them or for myself—but I do know that it feels like a gift for both of us.

Occasionally my efforts to make learning a celebration fall on deaf ears. One undergraduate student in my classroom management course spent the term scrutinizing the use of positive rewards and recognition in the classroom. She would frequently roll her eyes at my efforts to use raffle tickets, certificates, praise, and positive strategies to model celebration.

Finally, in my end-of-the-term tradition of conducting a Peer Awards Program, where the students and I present certificates of appreciation to one another, the class and I awarded this student with a Making a Difference award. She was stunned. At the end of class she came up to me and asked me for a favor. She asked if I would make a duplicate of the award to send to her father. Celebrating is a gift. Sometimes it has to be unwrapped and given away to have its greatest value.

Kris

RESOURCES

DuFour, R., & R. Eaker (1998). *Professional Learning Communities at Work: Best Practices for Enhancing Student Achievement.* Bloomington, Ind.: National Education Service.

ChartHouse Learning Mission. Retrieved August 12, 2004, from www.charthouse.com.

Connors, Neila. (2000). *If You Don't Feed the Teachers They Eat the Students: Guide to Success for Administrators and Teachers.* Nashville, Tenn.: Incentive.

Freiberg, K., and J. Freiberg (1996). *Nuts! Southwest Airlines' Crazy Recipe for Business and Personal Success.* New York: Broadway Books.

Kouzes, J., and B. Posner (1999). *Encouraging the Heart: A Leader's Guide to Rewarding and Recognizing Others.* San Francisco: Jossey-Bass.

Lundin, S., J. Christenson, & H. Paul (2002). *Fish Tales.* New York: Hyperion.

McNally, D. (1990). *Even Eagles Need a Push: Learning to Soar in a Changing World.* Eden Prairie, Minn.: Transform.

Rubin, H. (2002). *Collaborative Leadership: Developing Partnerships in Communities and Schools.* Thousands Oaks, Calif.: Corwin.

REFERENCES

Arnold, J., & C. Stevenson (1998). *Teachers' Teaming Handbook: A Middle Level Planning Guide.* Orlando, Fla.: Harcourt Brace.

Barnes, F., & M. Miller (2001, April). Data Analysis by Walking Around. *AASA Web Publications*, 58(4), 20–26.

Barth, R. (2001). *Learning by Heart.* San Francisco: Jossey-Bass.

Bell, C. (1996). *Managers as Mentors: Building Partnerships for Learning.* San Francisco: Berrett-Koehler.

Bernhardt, V. (2002). *The School Portfolio: A Comprehensive Framework for School Improvement.* Larchmont, N.Y.: Eye on Education.

Bolman, L., & R. Deal (2003). *Reframing Organizations: Artistry, Choice, and Leadership.* San Francisco: Jossey-Bass.

Brown, G., & B. Irby (1997). *The Principal Portfolio.* Thousand Oaks, Calif.: Corwin.

Campbell, D., P. Cignetti, B. Melenyzer, D. Nettles, & R. Wyman (2001). *How to Develop a Professional Portfolio.* Boston: Allyn & Bacon.

ChartHouse Learning Mission. Retrieved August 12, 2004, from www.charthouse.com.

Communities of Hope. *The Hope Foundation.* Retrieved September 19, 2004, from www.communitiesof hope.org.

Connors, N. (2000). *If You Don't Feed the Teachers They Eat the Students: Guide to Success for Administrators and Teachers.* Nashville, Tenn.: Incentive.

Costantino, P., & M. DeLorenzo (2002). *Developing a Professional Teaching Portfolio: A Guide for Success.* Boston: Allyn and Bacon.

Covey, S. (1990). *Principle Centered Leadership.* New York: Summit Books.

Covey, S., A. R. Merrill, & R. R. Merrill. (1994). *First Things First.* New York: Simon & Schuster.

Deal, T., & A. Kennedy (1982). *Corporate Cultures: The Rites and Rituals of Corporate Life.* Reading, Mass.: Addison-Wesley.

Deal, T., & K. Peterson (1999). *Shaping School Culture: The Heart of Leadership.* San Francisco: Jossey-Bass.

Deal, T., & K. Peterson. (2002). *Shaping School Culture Fieldbook.* San Francisco: Jossey-Bass.

Dietz, M. (2001). *Designing the School Leader's Portfolio.* Arlington Heights, Ill.: Skylight.

Downey, C., B. Steffy, F. English, L. Frase, & W. Poston (2004). *The Three-Minute Classroom Walk-Through: Changing School Supervisory Practice One Teacher at a Time.* Thousand Oaks, CA: Corwin.

DuFour, R., & R. Eaker (1998). *Professional Learning Communities at Work: Best Practices for Enhancing Student Achievement.* Bloomington, Ind.: National Education Service.

Dyer, W. (2004). *The Power of Intention: Learning to Co-create Your World Your Way.* Carlsbad, Calif.: Hay House.

Freiberg, K., & J. Freiberg (1996). *Nuts! Southwest Airlines' Crazy Recipe for Business and Personal Success.* New York: Broadway Books.

Fullan, M. (2001). *Leading in a Culture of Change.* San Francisco: Jossey-Bass.

Fullan, M. (2004). *Leading in a Culture of Change: Personal Action Guide and Workbook.* San Francisco: Jossey-Bass.

Ginsberg, M., & D. Murphy (2002, May). How Walkthroughs Open Doors. *Educational Leadership*.

Green, R. L. (2001). *Practicing the Art of Leadership: A Problem-Based Approach to Implementing the ISLLC Standards*. Columbus, Ohio: Prentice Hall.

Heller, D. (2004). *Teachers Wanted: Attracting and Retaining Good Teachers*. Alexandria, Va.: ASCD.

Huang, A. C., & J. Lynch (1995). *Mentoring: The TAO of Giving and Receiving Wisdom*. San Francisco: HarperSanFrancisco.

Interstate Consortium on School Leadership. *Council of Chief State School Officers*. Retrieved September 21, 2005, from www.ccsso.org.

Jackson, P., & H. Delehanty (1995). *Sacred Hoops: Spiritual Lessons of a Hardwood Warrior*. New York: Hyperion.

Jones, L. (1998). *The Path: Creating Your Mission Statement for Work and for Life*. New York: Hyperion.

Katzenbach, J., & D. Smith (1993). *The Wisdom of Teams: Creating the High Performance Organization*. New York: HarperCollins.

Kelleher, J. (2002, October). Encouraging Reflective Practice. *Principal Leadership*, 3(2), 20–23.

Kouzes, J., & B. Posner (1995). *The Leadership Challenge*. San Francisco: Jossey-Bass.

Kouzes, J., & B. Posner (1999). *Encouraging the Heart: A Leader's Guide to Rewarding and Recognizing Others*. San Francisco: Jossey-Bass.

Leithwood, K., D. Jantzi, & R. Steinbach (1999). *Changing Leadership for Changing Times*. Philadelphia: Open University Press.

Looper, S., and R. Wyatt (1999). *So You Have to Have a Portfolio: A Teacher's Guide to Preparation and Presentation*. Thousand Oaks, Calif.: Corwin.

Lundin, S., J. Christenson, & H. Paul (2002). *Fish Tales*. New York: Hyperion.

Martin-Kniep, G. (1999). *Capturing the Wisdom of Practice: Professional Portfolios for Educators*. Alexandria, Va.: ASCD.

Maxwell, J. (1993). *Developing the Leader within You*. Nashville, Tenn.: Injoy.

Maxwell, J. (1995). *Developing the Leaders around You: How to Help Others Reach Their Full Potential*. Nashville, Tenn.: Thomas Nelson.

Maxwell, J. (1999). *The 21 Indispensable Qualities of a Leader: Becoming the Person Others Will Want to Follow*. Nashville, Tenn.: Maxwell Motivational.

Maxwell, J. (2001a). *Developing the Leader within You Workbook*. Nashville, Tenn.: Injoy.

Maxwell, J. (2001b). *The 17 Indisputable Laws of Teamwork*. Nashville, Tenn.: Thomas Nelson.

Maxwell, J. (2002). *Your Road Map for Success*. Nashville, Tenn.: Maxwell Motivation.

McGraw, P. (2001). *Self Matters: Creating Your Life from the Inside Out*. New York: Free Press.

McNally, D. (1990). *Even Eagles Need a Push: Learning to Soar in a Changing World*. Eden Prairie, Minn.: Transform.

Mission Statement Builder. *Franklin Covey*. Retrieved September 21, 2004, from www.franklincovey.com.

Nanus, B. (1992). *Visionary Leadership*. San Francisco: Jossey-Bass.

Palmer, P. (1998). *The Courage to Teach*. San Francisco: Jossey-Bass.

Portfolio Instructions. *National Board for Professional Teaching Standards*. Retrieved April 13, 2004, from www.nbpts.org.

President's Council on Physical Fitness and Sports (n.d.). *Fitness Fundamentals*. Retrieved January 18, 2004, from www.hoptechno.com/book11.htm.

Professional Learning Communities. *National Education Service*. Retrieved September 19, 2004, from www.solution-tree.com.

Reeves, D. (2004). *Assessing Educational Leaders: Evaluating Performance for Improved Individual and Organizational Results*. Thousands Oaks, Calif.: Corwin.

Resnick, L. (1995). From Aptitude to Effort: A New Foundation for Our Schools. *Daedalus*, 11(4), 55–62.

Richardson, J. (2001, October/November). Seeing through New Eyes. *Tools for Schools*.

Robbins, P., & H. Alvy (1995). *The Principal's Companion: Strategies and Hints to Make the Job Easier*. Thousand Oaks, Calif.: Corwin.

Rubin, H. (2002). *Collaborative Leadership: Developing Effective Partnerships in Communities and Schools.* Thousand Oaks, Calif.: Corwin.

Scholtes, P. (1988). *The Team Handbook.* Madison, Wis.: Joiner.

Sergiovanni, T. J. (1996). *Moral Leadership: Getting to the Heart of School Improvement.* San Francisco: Jossey-Bass.

Sergiovanni, T. J. (2001). *The Principalship: A Reflective Practice Perspective.* 4th edition. Boston: Allyn and Bacon.

Senge, P. (1990). The *Fifth Discipline: The Art and Practice of a Learning Organization.* New York: Doubleday.

Senge, P., A. Kleiner, C. Roberts, R. Ross, & B. Smith (1994). *The Fifth Discipline Fieldbook: Strategies and Tools for Building a Learning Organization.* New York: Doubleday.

Wheatley, M. (2002). *Turning to One Another: Simple Conversations to Restore Hope to the Future.* San Francisco: Berrett-Koehler.

Wilmore, E. (2002). *Principal Leadership: Applying the New Educational Leadership Constituent Council (ELCC) Standards.* Thousand Oaks, Calif.: Corwin.

Wilmore, E., & C. Thomas (2001, Spring). The New Century: Is it Too Late for Transformational Leadership? *Educational Horizons,* Pi Lambda Theta, 79(3), 115–23.

York-Barr, J., W. Sommers, G. Ghere, & J. Montie (2001). *Reflective Practice to Improve Schools: An Action Guide for Educators.* Thousand Oaks, Calif.: Corwin.

Zachary, L. (2000). *The Mentor's Guide: Facilitating Effective Learning Relationships.* San Francisco: Jossey-Bass.

INDEX

ABOUT THE AUTHORS

Kristine Servais has been a middle school and elementary teacher, middle school assistant principal and principal, the director of field experiences for preservice teachers, and presently is an assistant professor in educational leadership. The middle school of which she was principal was recognized as a National Blue Ribbon School of Excellence. Kristine has studied school principals and, in particular, transformational leadership as a means for schools to collaboratively create a community of learners. Her most recent work has included the study of the roles, responsibilities, and relationships of the principal as a transformational leader in school–university partnerships.

Kellie Sanders has been a middle school teacher for ten years and has been active in many roles as a school leader. She has a master's degree in educational administration. Kellie completed her first administrative position as an assistant principal at an urban middle school and is presently in her third year as an elementary school principal.